Cool
Jump-Rope
Tricks
You Can Do!

David Fisher
The Rope Warrior

Meadowbrook Press
Distributed by Simon & Schuster
New York, NY

Library of Congress Cataloging-in-Publication Data

Fisher, David.
  Cool jump-rope tricks you can do / by David Fisher.
     pages cm.
  ISBN 978-1-4814-1231-5 (alk. paper)
1. Rope skipping--Juvenile literature. 2. Jump rope rhymes--Juvenile literature. I. Title.
  GV498.F57 2014
  796.2--dc23
                          2014015158

434 4712

Creative Director: Tamara JM Peterson
Copy Editor and Proofreader: Doug McNair
Models: Orly Hirsch, Adam Hirsch, Jeremiah Eunice, Vanya Gupta, Audrey Kim, Eliana Strauss, Felix Fisher, Max Fisher, and David Fisher
Photographer: Joe Arce, Starstruck Foto
Illustrator: Jeff Felson

Published by
Meadowbrook Press
6110 Blue Circle Drive, Suite 237
Minnetonka, Minnesota 55343
www.meadowbrookpress.com

BOOK TRADE DISTRIBUTION by
Simon & Schuster, a division of Simon & Schuster, Inc.
1230 Avenue of the Americas
New York, New York 10020

18 17 16 15 14   1 2 3 4 5 6 7 8 9 10

Printed in the United States of America

Dedication

To my beautiful wife, Renee.
Without your hard work and support, I wouldn't get
to continue having the greatest job in the world.

And to all of our men and women who serve in our armed forces.
You provide all of us who live in this blessed country
the safety and freedom to pursue our dreams.

Bloopers, stories, and fun facts from The Rope Warrior... pages 29, 51, and 71

Table of Contents

Introduction

Welcome to "Cool Jump-Rope Tricks You Can Do!" And good for you for starting at the beginning and reading the introduction! Most people probably jumped (no pun intended) right into the picture section, but it is especially important to read the "Look Before You Leap" section. When you do move into the picture section, you will notice that the majority of the skills included in this book are for beginners. That's because beginners form the largest group of jumpers and because every PE teacher wants new skills and tricks for beginners and non-jumpers. Beginner skills and tricks do not require great athletic ability or previous jump-rope experience. Having said that, this book also includes beginner tricks that will interest intermediate and advanced jumpers who have not seen such tricks before. In addition, we include some new, higher-level tricks that will challenge even advanced jumpers.

A Note to Parents and Teachers:

This book is written to give jump-rope enthusiasts of all ages the building blocks for creating their own jump-rope tricks and routines and to provide sample skills and tricks for them to try. I usually use the terms *skills* and *tricks* interchangeably, but for the purposes of this book, the *skills* in any category will be the building blocks for the *tricks* in the following chapter.

Most of the pages in this book present individual rope techniques. We also provide a sampling of skills and tricks for two people using one rope. Beginning, intermediate, and advanced jumpers can find skills to try throughout the book. The skills or tricks in each chapter are presented by level of difficulty, from easiest to hardest—they are marked as "Beginner," "Intermediate," or "Advanced." The presentation of each technique includes detailed step-by-step instructions plus verbal cues to assist jumpers. I've included some classic jump-rope techniques and some of my new favorite tricks. You may also find that some beginner tricks that appear later in the book are easier than tricks taught in earlier chapters.

All along the way, there are
helpful hints from me,
The Rope Warrior!

Look Before You Leap

In this chapter, we will discuss everything you need to do and know before you get started. Topics include an introduction to jumping rope, safety, types of ropes, the appropriate length of a rope, jumping surfaces, making mistakes, warming up, and proper jumping form.

Welcome to Cool Jump-Rope Tricks You Can Do!

The techniques presented in this book comprise a combination of rope jumping, rhythmic gymnastics, dance, and martial arts. This program is designed to be as inclusive as possible and to give rope-jumping enthusiasts of all ages and abilities a lot of new skills and tricks to try. Originally, when I thought about titles and subtitles for the book, I considered phrases like "The Complete Book of" and "Everything You Wanted to Know About." But all such phrases imply a finite number of tricks. The fact is that the skills included in this book represent a small fraction of the tricks that I knew at the time I wrote this and an even smaller fraction of the tricks that I know are possible. The bottom line is that no matter how good you are and how many tricks you know, there are always new skills to learn and new ideas to share with other people.

Safety

Please consult a physician before beginning any exercise program.

If you are jumping with or near others, make sure that you are spread out enough so that you are not too close to anyone else; you obviously don't want to get hit or hit anyone else with your rope. When you jump, work on landing softly. You do this by landing on the balls of your feet, bringing the weight back toward your heels, and bending your knees as you land. You want to cushion the impact as much as possible. I often tell students, "You want to hear the rope and not your feet." Please follow the step-by-step instructions to help prevent injury, and please also take note of special safety tips on selected tricks.

Selecting a Jump Rope

The first thing that you need to do is pick out a jump rope. In my program, we use cloth ropes (with knots for handles), speed ropes, and segmented (or beaded) ropes.

Cloth ropes are used for learning tricks in which one or more of the handles are released. (It's never fun getting hit with a handle.) Longer cloth ropes (14–16 feet) are used for teaching double Dutch. The weight of a double-Dutch cloth rope allows for more turner control (especially outside), and if a beginning double-Dutch jumper accidentally lands on a cloth rope, there is less chance of a wipeout.

Speed ropes are my preferred ropes for teaching single-rope tricks. They cut through the air for speed jumping and power tricks, they don't pinch your skin on an arm wrap, and getting hit with a speed rope hurts less than getting hit with a segmented rope.

Segmented ropes are used for performances and workshop instruction. They are easier for an audience or a PE class to see, they hold their shape well, and they go fast enough to do most power tricks.

If you do not purchase an official* Rope Warrior rope, you may still be able to do many of the tricks in this book. However, ropes that don't turn well, tangle easily, or are too light or too heavy only make things more difficult. In addition, Rope Warrior ropes have the perfect balance between rope weight and handle weight that you need for release moves.

As a general rule, when you step on the middle of the jump rope, the handles should come up to about shoulder height. A shorter rope is better for speed jumping since it gives less air resistance, while a long rope makes crossing tricks easier to learn. To minimize misses, it is always better to have a rope that is a little too long rather than a little to short. In addition, you can always put some knots below the handle to shorten a speed rope. See the chart below for selecting a rope length.

Jumper's Height	Suggested Rope Length
Under 4'0"	6 feet long
4'0" to 4'9"	7 feet long
4'9" to 5'3"	8 feet long
5'3" to 5'10"	9 feet long
5'10" to 6'5"	10 feet long
6'5"+	11 feet long

*For more information about official Rope Warrior ropes, see page 152.

Jumping Surfaces

I have performed and taught all over the world, and I am always astonished (but never surprised) when a site coordinator selects a floor surface that is going to make my job more difficult. So here they are, in order of preference: my top-ten floor surfaces:

#1 Suspended Wood Floor: This surface is smooth and flat, it helps absorb impact, and it returns the energy to help you rebound. IT IS IDEAL FOR ROPE JUMPING.

#2 Solid Wood Floor: This surface is also smooth and flat, but it's not as springy as a suspended wood floor.

#3 Sport Court: This surface consists of solid floor tiles linked together. It's not quite as smooth as wood, but it's still an excellent alternative.

#4 Polyurethane Floor: This surface is smooth and flat, and it provides decent cushioning for a workout. But the rope doesn't slide quite as well on this surface.

#5 Carpeting: There is still some cushioning, but the rope tends to bounce off of the carpet and into your feet more often.

#6 Hard Tile Floor: Unfortunately, there are still way too many elementary schools with this type of flooring. It's very unforgiving and hard on the joints. I do not recommend prolonged periods of jumping on this type of floor.

#7 Blacktop: This surface is all right for recess but not for extended workouts.

#8 Dirt: Yes, I've performed on dirt—and I looked like Pigpen (that's a *Peanuts* reference), dust cloud and all.

#9 Paved Streets: In addition to the problem of constantly looking around for cars, this surface is hard and rough; there will be extra wear and tear on your joints and jump rope. However, jumping on paved streets is an unfortunate necessity during parade performances. I recommend trying to get a spot in the parade line *in front* of the horses!

#10 Grass: The rope will continuously be caught in or slowed by the grass, making it very difficult to jump.

Solutions: The harder the surface that you are jumping on, the more important it becomes to have shoes with good cushioning in the forefoot. Also, a thin (not too squishy) mat can be used on top of a hard surface. Using a mat is also a good idea for jumping rope at home. It can be placed on top of a carpet or in a garage or driveway. Make sure that the mat is large enough that the rope won't hit an edge while you are jumping.

Making Mistakes

If you keep an open mind, practice, are ready to make mistakes (i.e., learn), and have some faith in your instructor (I am recognized by *Ripley's Believe It or Not!* as the World's Best Rope Jumper, and I'm told that I'm an even better teacher), then I promise that you'll be having fun, keeping fit, and showing off to your friends in no time!

Warm-up

Whether you are designing a workout, a PE class, or a routine of funtastic jump rope tricks, you will want to make sure that your body is prepared for the work it will be asked to do. Before any show or workout, I always like to do some light jumping and some running in place to elevate my heart rate and get the blood flowing. I also do some range-of-motion and stretching exercises to prevent my muscles from tightening.

Proper Jumping Form

Let's go through a little exercise without the jump rope. If you are standing in front of a mirror, great—if not, try to find one next time. Keep your head up, shoulders down, elbows in, and arms and upper body relaxed. Now with your elbows in and your palms facing forward, start turning your wrists like you are scrambling eggs with a fork, one on each side. You want to restrict your arm movement as much as possible and let your wrists and your imaginary rope do most of the work for you. Take a look at your hands. Is your weak hand making the same kind of circle or oval shape that your strong hand is making? Are your elbows still in?

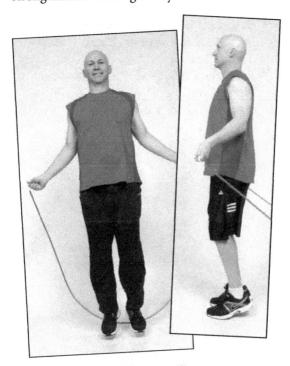

Now as the imaginary rope starts to come down, lift your heels off the ground by pushing down on the balls of your feet and then bring your heels back down again (you are not jumping yet). Do this about ten times. Now start to add a little knee bend when your heels come down. Do that about ten times as well. Your knees should track straight over your feet and should not go out past your toes. Now push just a little harder on your heel lifts so that you make a little jump each time the imaginary rope comes down, followed immediately by landing on the balls of your feet. Let the weight come back toward your heels and then bend your knees as before, to cushion the impact as much as possible. Are you landing softly? Are your elbows still in? Is your head up, and is your upper body relaxed?

Non-Jumping Skills

Here is a step-by-step breakdown of skills for all you non-jumpers.

These skills are designed to help beginners like you get a
feel for the rope without worrying about tripping over it.
Everybody be ready to make a lot of mistakes!

Hands In and Out
(Beginner)

All hands on deck! Here is a little warm-up to get us going.

Helpful Hint:
The plank position is just like a starting push-up position, except that your hands are a little closer together.

Don't wear yourself out on this first skill—we're just getting started!

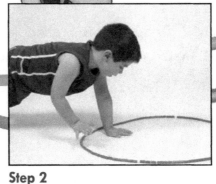

Step 1
Lay your jump rope on the ground and make it into a big circle by touching the ends together.

Step 2
Get in a plank position with your hands just outside the circle and begin to walk your hands into the circle—one at a time. Remain in the plank position and walk your hands out of the circle.

Step 3
Repeat the pattern: In/In, Out/Out

Verbal cues: in, in, out, out

Feet In and Out
(Beginner)

Now let's get our legs warmed up. If in the beginning, it is too tiring to do 10 sets of each pattern, start with fewer sets and work your way up!

Helpful Hint:
Make sure that you are **not** jogging over your handles. Stay just on the outside of the circle but move as far away from the handles as you can.

Step 1
In/Out, In/Out: Lay your jump rope on the ground and make it into a big circle by touching the ends together. Start with both feet outside the circle and face the circle. Jog into the circle with your left foot, then jog out of the circle with your right foot (repeat 10x).

Step 2
In/In, Out/Out: Jog into the circle with your left foot, jog into the circle with your right foot, jog out of the circle with your left foot, and jog out of the circle with your right foot (repeat 10x).

Step 3
In/In/In, Out/Out/Out: Jog into the circle with your left foot, jog into the circle with your right foot, make a third jog in the circle on your left foot, then jog out of the circle with your right foot, jog out of the circle with your left foot, and then make a third jog out of the circle with your right foot (repeat 10x).

Verbal cues: in, out (repeat 10x)   in, in, out, out (10x)   in, in, in, out, out, out (10x)

Forward Circle
(Beginner)

These first few rope skills are designed to give you a good feel for the rope. Be patient, keep trying, and you'll be jumping before you know it!

Helpful Hint:
Try this skill with your eyes closed. If you are making a good circle, you should be able to feel where the rope is without looking at it.

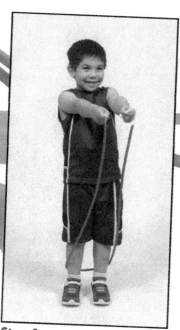

Step 1
Start with the rope at your heels, tug (bring your hands forward), and tap your fists together.

Step 2
Bring both hands down, back, and around so that the middle of the rope makes a forward circle all the way around you.

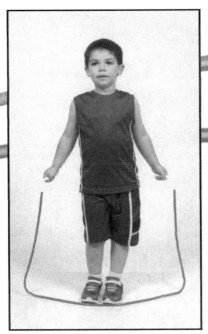

Step 3
Let the rope hit your feet, step over, and repeat steps 1–3.

Can you feel where the rope is without looking at it? Wait a minute... how can you read this if your eyes are closed?!?

Verbal cues: rope at heels   tug and tap   make a circle   step over

Cool Jump-Rope Tricks You Can Do

Backward Circle
(Beginner)

Some of you may find it easier to make good **backward** circles.

Helpful Hint:
Try this one with your eyes closed, too.

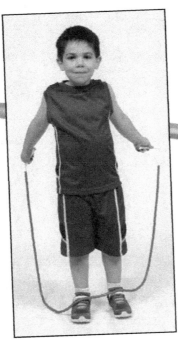

Step 1
Start with the middle of the rope on top of your feet and then bring your arms back.

Step 2
Swing the rope backward over your head (make a backward circle).

Step 3
Let the rope hit your heels, then step backward over the rope. Repeat steps 1, 2, and 3.

Forward Mousetrap
(Beginner)

Here's a non-jumping skill that is still a good warm-up for your lower leg muscles.

Helpful Hint:
Once you get the hang of it, it will feel like you are rocking back and forth from your toes to your heels.

Step 1
Tug and tap, then bring both hands down, back, and around so that the middle of the rope starts to make a circle all the way around you.

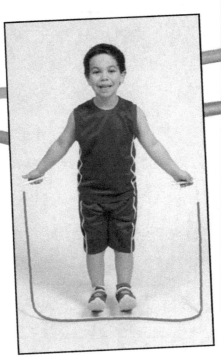

Step 2
As the rope comes over your head, lift your toes and then trap the rope underneath your feet by lowering your toes.

Step 3
Lift your heels and bring your hands down, back, and around again. Repeat steps 2 and 3.

See how quickly you can catch and release!

Backward Mousetrap
(Beginner)

Try the Mousetrap with the rope going backward this time.

Helpful Hint:
As you rock back and forth, your knees always stay a little bit bent, and your hips go forward and backward.

Step 1
Start with the middle of the rope on top of your feet and then bring your arms back. Make a backward circle with the rope, then lift your heels as the rope goes behind you.

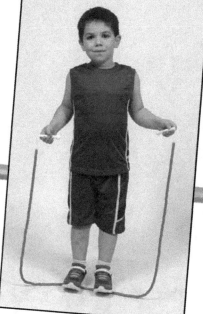

Step 2
Trap the rope underneath your feet by lowering your heels.

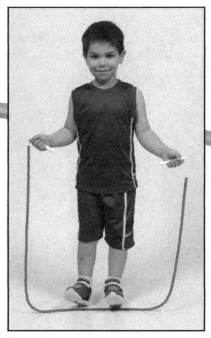

Step 3
Lift your toes, make another backward circle with the rope, lift your heels, and repeat steps 2 and 3.

Verbal cues: rope at toes   backward circle   lift your heels   catch   release

1-Hand Side Swing
(Beginner)

You can use this skill to practice footwork skills without tripping over the rope.

Helpful Hint:
While you are doing a 1-Hand Side Swing, pretend that you are turning one handle in each hand and practice that good jumping form!

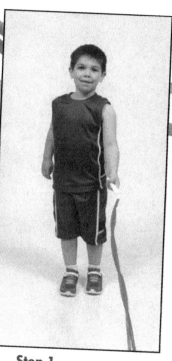

Step 1
Place both handles in your right hand.

Step 2
Turn the rope at your side. Make sure that the middle of the rope hits the ground on every swing.

Step 3
Repeat steps 1 and 2 using your left hand.

2-Hand Open Side Swing
(Beginner)

You will use the side-swing part (Step 2) of this skill a lot, when you go from one trick to another.

Helpful Hint:
The rope might tangle a little on this because it's usually better to go from an open side swing to a crossed side swing, or to a crossed jump.

Step 1
Start with the rope at your heels. Tug and tap. Then bring both hands down, back, and around so that the middle of the rope starts to make a forward circle all the way around you. Start to bring your left hand over to your right side.

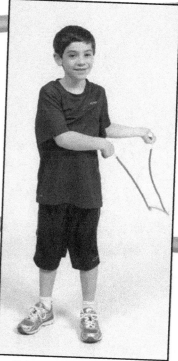

Step 2
Do an **open** side swing on your right side.

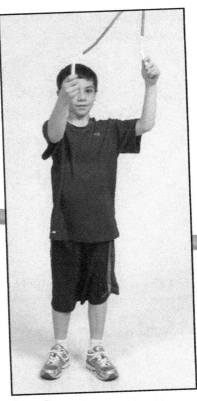

Step 3
Open your hands and let the rope hit your feet—no jumping yet.
Variation: Try an open side swing on the left (with your left hand farther out than your right hand.)

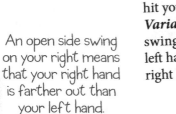

An open side swing on your right means that your right hand is farther out than your left hand.

Verbal cues: tug and tap   circle   swing both on the right   open

2-Hand Crossed Side Swing
(Beginner)

I hope that you haven't forgotten the 2-Hand Open Side Swing, because you will use these two tricks together, often.

Helpful Hint:
There doesn't need to be a huge distance between your hands on this 2-Hand Crossed Side Swing, but your hands do need to be crossed.

Step 1
Start with the rope at your heels. Tug and tap. Then bring both hands down, back, and around so that the middle of the rope starts to make a circle all the way around you. Start to bring your left hand over to your right side.

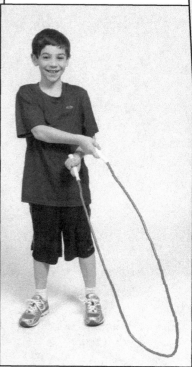

Step 2
Get your left hand farther out to your right than your right hand, then do a crossed side swing on your right side.

Step 3
Open your hands and let the rope hit your feet—no jumping yet.
Variation: Try a crossed side swing on your left (with your right hand farther out to your left than your left hand.)

| Verbal cues: | tug and tap | circle | crossed side swing on the right | open |

1, 2, 3 Switch
(Beginner)

Now it's time to take that 1-hand side swing and jazz it up a bit!

Helpful Hint:
Swing the rope **forward**, not backward, and make sure the middle of the rope hits the ground on each swing.

Step 1
Start with both handles in your right hand. Swing the rope on your right side and say, "1, 2, 3."

Step 2
As you say the word "switch," pass both handles from your right hand to your left hand.

Step 3
Swing the rope on your left side.
Variation: Start with the rope in your left hand and switch to your right hand.

Verbal cues: 1, 2, 3   switch

1, 2, 3
Under
(Beginner)

This time, you are going to switch hands under your knee!

Helpful Hint:
Swing the rope **forward**, not backward, and make sure the middle of the rope hits the ground with each swing.

Step 1
Start with both handles in your right hand. Swing the rope on your side and say, "1, 2, 3."

Step 2
Lift your left knee as you say the word "under" and pass both handles from your right hand to your left hand. Make the switch **under** your left knee.

Step 3
Swing the rope on your left side. *Variation:* Start with the rope in your left hand and switch under your right knee.

Verbal cues: 1, 2, 3   under

Behind-the-Back Pass
(Beginner)

Here is another side-swing variation for you to try.

Helpful Hint:
Keep a nice, **slow**, even tempo on this one.

Step 1
Put both handles in your right hand and do a 1-hand side swing on your right side.

Step 2
As the rope starts to come down, put your left hand behind your back and switch the handles to your left hand.

Step 3
Immediately bring your left hand to your left side and continue doing side swings on your left side.
Variation: Start with the rope in your left hand and switch behind your back to your right hand.

Verbal cues: 1, 2, 3   behind the back

Under Under
(Beginner)

You'll need quick hands and quick knees for this one!

Helpful Hint:
Do this trick slowly until you get the hang of it.

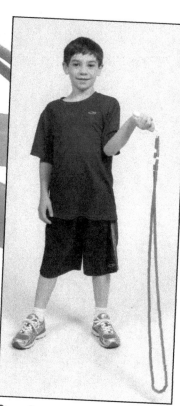

Step 1
Do a 1-hand side swing on your right side and count, "1, 2, 3."

Step 2
As the rope is coming down, you say, "Under," lift your left knee, and pass both handles under your left leg from your right hand to your left hand.

Step 3
Immediately bring your left knee down, lift your right knee up, say, "Under" again, and pass the handles back to your right hand, under your right leg.
Variation: Try the same trick, but start in your **left** hand.

| Verbal cues: | 1, 2, 3 | under | under |

Cool Jump-Rope Tricks You Can Do

Helicopter
(Beginner)

Practice this one and you will be ready for the partner jumping trick on page 128.

Make sure that there is no one near you when you try this one!

Helpful Hint:
When the rope is above your head, always keep your arm next to your head. The farther your arm gets away from your head, the more likely you are to get hit by the rope.

Step 1
Hold both handles in one hand. Hold your hand high above your head and slowly spin the rope like a helicopter.

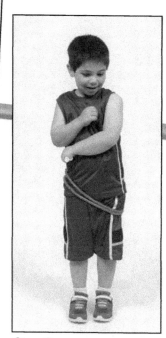

Step 2
Continue spinning, then drop your hand down. Let the rope wrap around your legs.

Step 3
As soon as the rope is fully wrapped around your legs, lift your hand back up high in the air. The rope will unwrap and should now be spinning above your head in the opposite direction. Repeat steps 2 and 3.

Verbal cues: helicopter drop down unwrap back up high

Non-Jumping Skills

Non-Jumping Tricks

Once you have some basic non-jumping skills down, it's time to try some tricks!
These include wraps, step-throughs, manipulations, and tosses.
These funtastic tricks are listed in order from easiest to hardest.

Body Wrap
(Beginner)

Your first trick!
Are you excited?
Try each trick step-by-step
and be ready to
practice a lot!

Helpful Hint:
Keep your lower hand still and
let your top hand do all of the
wrapping and unwrapping.

If you learn one trick on your
first day, you are one trick ahead
of where I was on my first day!

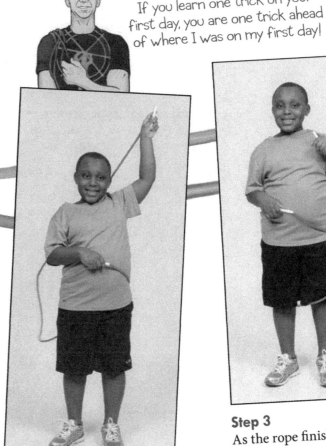

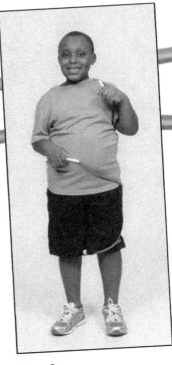

Step 1
Start with the rope in front,
one handle in each hand, with
your right hand up high and
your left hand down by your
belly button.

Step 2
Bring your right hand back and
around your head. Let the rope
begin to wrap around you.

Step 3
As the rope finishes wrapping,
bring your right hand down so
that the rope does not hit your
face. Then unwrap.

Verbal cues: rope in front   right hand up left hand down   back behind your head   wrap   unwrap

Arm Wrap
(Beginner)

Here is a great non-jumping trick to have in your routine. It keeps the rope moving, gives you a moment to catch your breath, and easily flows right back into a jumping trick.

Helpful Hint:
Use your shoulder muscles to make circles with your straight arm when wrapping or unwrapping.

Step 1
Hold the rope in front of you, with one handle in each hand. Put your right hand straight out and your left hand on your right shoulder.

Step 2
Keep your right arm straight and swing the rope back and forth like a swing. Keep swinging higher.

Step 3
Swing the rope forward over your arm. Continue wrapping the rope **forward** on your straight right arm. After the rope is fully wrapped, fully unwrap (the rope is going backward) and then immediately continue wrapping backward.

Verbal cues: rope in front   right arm out   hand on shoulder   swing   wrap   unwrap   wrap again

Open Step-Through
(Beginner)

A step-through is one way to get your feet over the rope without jumping.

Helpful Hint:
Keep your lower hand still and let your upper hand bring the rope around.

Make sure to always pick up your feet in front of you when you step over and step out.

Step 1
Hold the rope in front of you with your right hand up and your left hand down.

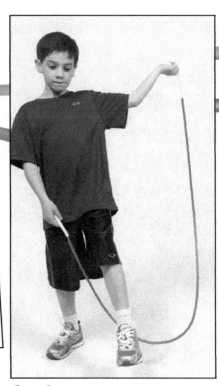

Step 2
Step over the rope with your right foot and begin to bring your right hand back and around your head.

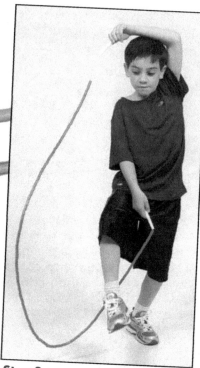

Step 3
As your right hand comes around to the front, pick up your left foot and angle it as you step out of the rope.
Variation: Try this trick again with your **left** hand up, and step over with your **left** foot first.

Verbal cues: rope in front   right hand up/left hand down   step over   step out

If you want to really make this one look fancy, keep your legs straight and point your toes when you step over and step out.

Spinning Step-Through
(Beginner)

This trick is the same as an Open Step-Through, except that you turn your body as you step over and step out.

Helpful Hint:
If you are stepping over with your **right** foot first, make sure that you are spinning to the **right**.

Step 1
Hold the rope in front of you with your right hand up and your left hand down.

Step 2
Step over the rope with your right foot and begin to turn to the right as you bring your right hand back and around your head.

Step 3
As your right hand comes around to the front, keep turning your body to the right and step out with your left foot.
Variation: Try this trick again with your **left** hand up, and step over with your **left** foot first as you turn your body to the **left**.

Verbal cues: step over with the right, turn to the right   step out with the left, turn to the right

Rope Toss
(Beginner)

Tossing the rope is the easy part. Practice your tosses so that you can eventually wrap, catch, or jump the rope when it comes down.

Helpful Hint:
Pretend that you are facing a high wall that is a few feet in front of you. Try to toss your rope so that it will hit **flat** at the top part of the wall and then slide along the wall as it comes down.

Step 1
Put both handles in your right hand. Spin the rope **clockwise** in front of you like an airplane propeller. As the rope is coming down, bring your hand down.

Step 2
Immediately bring your hand up and release the rope.

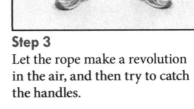

Step 3
Let the rope make a revolution in the air, and then try to catch the handles.

Tossing the rope should feel like you are tossing a tennis ball for a serve.

Verbal cues: both handles in your right hand   clockwise airplane propeller   toss

1-Hand Figure 8
(Beginner)

We are taking one you know (1-Hand Side Swing, page 12) and one you don't know yet (Front Cross Side Swing, page 58) and alternating them.

Helpful Hint:
Your hand will make a sideways figure 8, or an infinity sign.

Step 1
With both handles in your right hand, do a side swing on your right side and then start to bring your right hand to your left side.

Step 2
Do one side swing on your left side.

Step 3
Then immediately bring your right hand back to your right side. Continue alternating right, left, right, left, etc.

Verbal cues: both handles in one hand   swing on the right   swing on the left   swing on the right

2-Hand Figure 8
(Beginner)

The lead hand will always be the outside hand on either side swing and will make the bigger infinity sign.

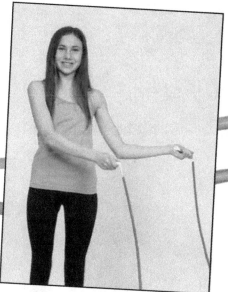

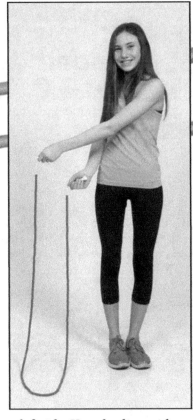

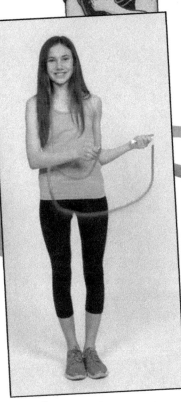

You would think that this trick would be just like a 1-Hand Figure 8 except that you put one handle in each hand. Try that first. I think you will find that you naturally lead with one hand or the other. We want you to learn how to lead with either hand.

Helpful Hint:
Don't read the paragraph above. It will probably confuse you. ☺

Step 1
Start with the rope at your heels. Tug, tap, and put your fists together. Bring both hands down, back, and around so that the rope goes over your head. Start to bring your left hand over to your right side.

Step 2
Do one **open** side swing on your right side.

Step 3
Start to bring both hands to your left side. Keep leading with your right hand and do a **crossed** side swing on your left side (your right hand will be farther out than your left hand), then start to bring both hands to your right side. Repeat steps 2 and 3. (I realize that you're in an infinite loop, so feel free to stop once you have the hang of it.)
Variation: Now try a **left-hand** lead by doing an open side swing on your left side and a crossed side swing on your right side.

Verbal cues: heels, tug, tap   circle   open side swing   crossed side swing

Bloopers, Stories, and Fun Facts

Funny Story:
As I was leaving a school after a performance, a kindergarten teacher and one of her students approached me.

"Lindsey wanted to meet you," the teacher said.

I shook hands with Lindsey, a shy, little red-haired five year old who continued to clutch her teacher's hand and partially hide behind her. Then in the smallest of voices, Lindsey proclaimed, "I tink I know why you're The Rope Worrier!"

"Why is that?" I asked.

"'Cause you swing da rope sooo fast you're worried it's gonna hit you… that's why you're The Rope Worrier!"

Fun Fact:
The part of the rope that moves the fastest when you're jumping is the middle of the rope. It makes the biggest circle, so it has to travel the farthest in the same amount of time. The Rope Warrior's rope has been timed at speeds over 100 miles per hour!

Poetry in Motion… Not!

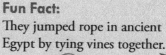

Too close for comfort!

TANGLED!   TANGLED AGAIN!

Goofy!

"When bad things happen to good facial expressions."

Fun Fact:
They jumped rope in ancient Egypt by tying vines together.

And NO, I didn't witness it personally—I'm not that old!

Double 8
(Intermediate)

Your first Intermediate trick! This one will take some practice, but it is a combination of Beginner tricks that you already know.

Helpful Hint:
In a Double 8, you do **two** side swings on each side. The first side swing on either side is always a **crossed** side swing.

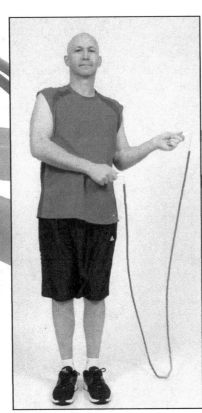

Step 1
Begin by doing a 2-Hand Figure 8, leading with your right hand (page 28). Take your last **single** side swing on your right side.

Step 2
Leading with your right hand, bring both hands over to your left side and do a crossed side swing on the left.

Step 3
Leave your hands on your left side and begin to uncross them for your second side swing on your left.

Verbal cues: cross   open

Cool Jump-Rope Tricks You Can Do

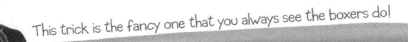

This trick is the fancy one that you always see the boxers do!

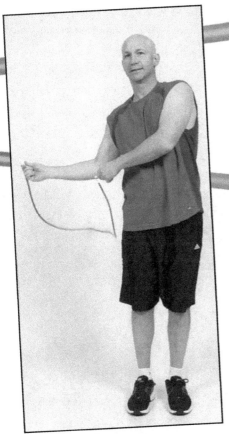

Step 4
Do an open side swing on your left.

Step 5
Now, leading with your LEFT hand, begin to bring both hands to your right side for a crossed side swing on the right.

Step 6
Do a crossed side swing on the right.

Step 7
Leave your hands on your right side and begin to uncross them for your second side swing on your right. Finish that open side swing on the right and repeat steps 2–7.

cross

open

The Houdini
(Intermediate)

This funtastic trick is going to make you look like you're all tangled up, but then at the last second, you'll escape—just like Houdini!

Helpful Hint:
Remember to step through from **the back** of the loop and keep your left hand all the way behind your back until the end of the trick.

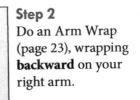

Step 2
Do an Arm Wrap (page 23), wrapping **backward** on your right arm.

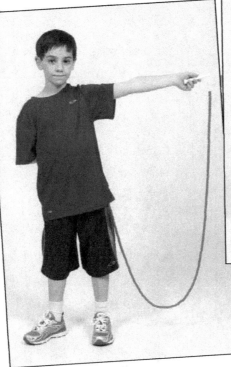

Step 1
Start with the rope behind you. Put your right arm straight out to the right and your left hand all the way behind your back.

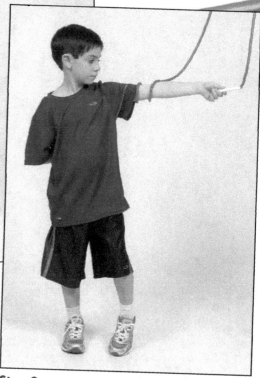

Step 3
Start unwrapping the rope; it should be turning **forward** now. Prepare to do a Spinning Step-Through (page 25) through the loop on your arm when it gets big enough.

Verbal cues: rope in back   right arm out   left hand behind   backward arm wrap   unwrap

Cool Jump-Rope Tricks You Can Do

Try to get the loop to come down at a diagonal toward your right foot when you step through it.

Step 4
Begin to step through from the **back** of the loop.

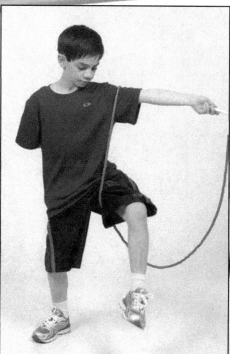

Step 5
As you step through the loop, think about turning your body as you start to bring your foot down.

Step 6
Keep turning your body as you bring your right hand back and around your head.

Step 7
Step out with your left foot and finish unwrapping.

Gentleman's Fake
(Intermediate)

It's a 2-Handed Figure 8 with one hand behind your back.

Helpful Hint:
You don't have to be able to do the Gentleman's Cross (page 80), but you might want to check it out before you try this one.

Before you try this trick with your rope, read through the steps and mime it in super-slow motion, without your rope.

Step 1
Start with the rope in back of you. Tug and tap.

Step 2
Then bring both hands down, back, and around so that the middle of the rope starts to make a circle all the way around you. Start to bring your right hand over to your left side.

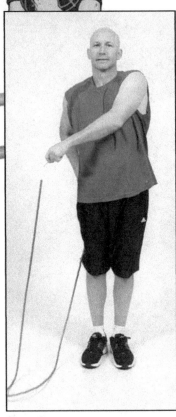

Step 3
As you swing the rope on the left, start to bring your left hand all the way behind your back.

Verbal cues: heels, tug, tap   circle   swing on the left   left hand behind

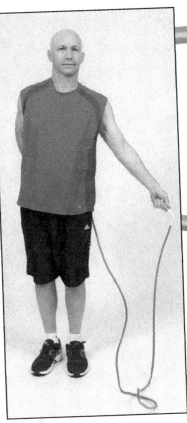

Step 4
Keep your right arm crossed in front of you, get the handle in your left hand (which is behind your back) as far to the right as possible, and let the loop come over your head.

Step 5
With your left hand still behind your back, start to uncross your right hand. Let the rope swing first, then have your right hand immediately follow it on the right side.

Step 6
Open up your arms and let the rope go over your head.

Step 7
Start to bring your right hand to your left side and repeat steps 3–7. *Variation:* Try the same trick, but swing on the right and put your right hand behind your back.

uncross right   open

Footwork Skills

These funtastic skills are distinguished by what you do with your feet.

First work on footwork skills, then try some footwork tricks,
and before you know it, you'll be dancing with the jump rope!

2-Foot Double Bounce,
2-Foot Single Bounce,
Hopping
(Beginner)

Here are your first three funtastic footwork skills. Remember to always land **softly** by landing on the balls of your feet and bringing the weight back toward your heels.

Helpful Hint:
First, try each of these footwork skills outside the rope while doing a 1-Hand Side Swing (page 12). Then try to jump inside the rope at half your normal jumping speed, and then slowly speed up once you master the skill.

Step 1
A **2-Foot Double Bounce**—or rebound jump—is used for partner jumping, long rope, and beginning single rope. For every turn of the rope, there is a big jump, little jump… big jump, little jump… big jump, little jump… etc…

Step 2
A **2-Foot Single Bounce**—or pogo-stick jump—is essential for most single-rope tricks and double Dutch. Do only one bounce, or jump, per turn; you hit the ground and go right back up (no rebound jump).

Step 3
Hopping occurs when you push off of one foot and land on the same foot. Hop on your left foot for four jumps, then switch to your right foot. Repeat.

I was so frustrated the first time I tried this skill. You might say I was hopping mad!

| Verbal cues: | big jump/little jump | pogo-stick jumps | hop |

Jogging
(Beginner)

Jogging in place with the jump rope is a great warm-up exercise. The skill pictured is one single-bounce jog for every one turn of the rope.

Helpful Hint:
Try not to bring your heels up in back when you jog. Just lift your foot slightly above where it was on the ground.

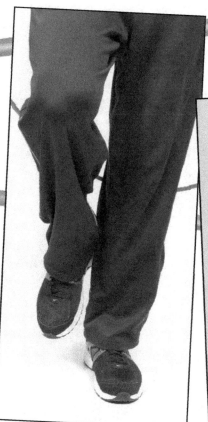

Step 1
Start with the rope behind you. As you swing it over your head, shift your weight to your right leg and lift your left foot.

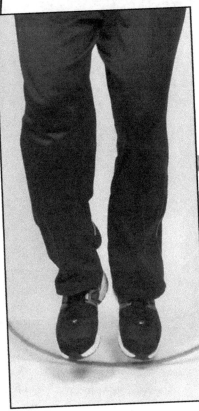

Step 2
As the rope comes down, push off of your right foot and get ready to land on your left foot.

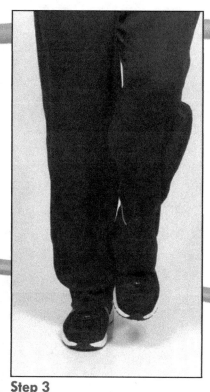

Step 3
Land on your left foot, then jog onto your right foot on the next turn of the rope. Continue the jogging pattern.
Variations: Try to slow your hands down and speed up your feet. Can you do two jogs per one turn of the rope? How about three? Four? How fast are your feet? What is your record?

Skipping
(Intermediate)

Skipping is effortless and fun. Why do we freak out when we add the jump rope?

Helpful Hint:
Make sure that the rope goes underneath you only on the hopping part.

Don't be skipping steps when learning the skipping steps.

Step 1
Start with the rope behind you. As you swing it over your head, shift your weight to your right leg, lift your left foot, and hop on your right foot as the rope goes under.

Step 2
After you land on your right foot, quickly shift the weight to your left leg and lift your right foot.

Step 3
Hop on your left foot as the rope goes under, quickly shift the weight to your right leg, lift your left foot, and continue the skipping pattern.

Verbal cues:	hop	step	hop	step/hop

Galloping
(Intermediate)

There are a lot of great variations on the gallop step that can be used for dance, sports training, and workouts. Even if you don't get this one right away, keep working at it!

Helpful Hint:
One leg does more work than the other when you gallop. Try to even out your gallops by switching your lead foot after a while.

Step 1
Start with the rope behind you. As you swing it over your head, shift your weight to your right leg and lift your left foot. Push off of your right foot and get ready to land on your left foot as the rope goes under.

Step 2
Jog onto your left foot as the rope goes under, and then quickly start to shift your weight to the right.

Step 3
Finish shifting the weight to your right foot, and then lift your left foot. Repeat the jog/step pattern.

Verbal cues: jog   step   jog/step

Footwork Tricks

Once you can do some of the basic footwork skills, try some of these fancy footwork tricks!

Work on footwork tricks the same way you learned footwork skills—first with side swings, and then at half your normal jumping speed until you master the trick.

Straddle Jumps
(Beginner)

Here is your first footwork trick. It's just like doing a jumping jack.

Helpful Hint:
You need to be able to do either a 2-Foot Double Bounce or a 2-Foot Single Bounce (preferred) to do Straddle Jumps.

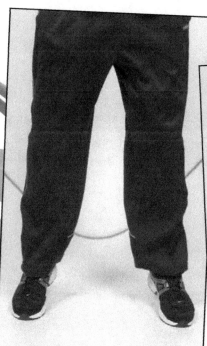

Step 1
Jump over the rope with your feet together and land with your feet apart.

Step 2
As the rope is coming down, jump with your feet apart and put them together as the rope goes under.

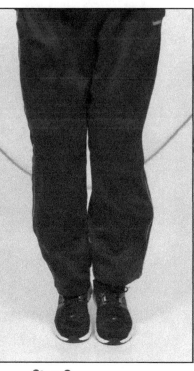

Step 3
Land with your feet together and repeat the apart/together pattern.

Verbal cues: apart   together   apart, together

Start with smaller foot movements until you get the hang of it. Don't spread your feet too wide or cross your feet too far.

Straddle Crosses
(Intermediate)

This is another variation on a 2-Foot Single Bounce.

Helpful Hint:
Try not to always cross the same foot in front. You want to alternate front feet.

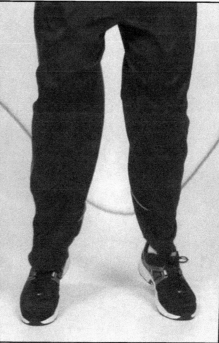

Step 1
Start by doing Straddle Jumps (page 44). When your feet are apart, jump and cross your right foot in front of your left foot as the rope goes underneath you. Land with your right foot in front of your left foot.

Step 2
As the rope is coming down again, jump with your feet crossed. The rope goes underneath, and then you land with your feet apart.

Step 3
On the next turn of the rope, jump with your feet apart and land with your left foot in front of your right foot this time. Repeat the cross/open pattern, alternating the front foot.

| Verbal cues: | cross | open | cross |

Toe Touch
(Intermediate)

Boxers use Toe Touches a lot when they are training; it helps them stay light on their feet. Can you "float like a butterfly?"

Helpful Hint:
Try a jogging step first. When you push off your foot and lift it, keep it by your other ankle and then slowly lower those foot lifts until your toes (on the lifted foot) barely touch the ground each time.

Step 1
Start with the rope in back. Shift almost all the weight to your right foot, but keep your left toe on the ground. As the rope comes down, lift your left foot and push off the right foot.

Step 2
Let the rope go under you, then land on your left foot.

Step 3
Tap your right toe. As the rope comes down again, lift your right foot and push off the left foot. Let the rope go under you, then land on your right foot and tap your left toe. Repeat the tap-right/tap-left pattern.

If you relax when you do Toe Touches, you will be able to jump for a long time. Try sticking your left hip out a little when you land on your left foot, and try sticking your right hip out a little when you land on your right foot.

Verbal cues: jog   tap right   tap left

If you're doing this one right, you're kicking butt!

Kick Backs
(Intermediate)

Our politicians all know the importance of Kick Backs. For you, the payoff will be stronger hamstring muscles.

Helpful Hint:
This is pictured as a right-foot, both-feet, left-foot, both-feet pattern. Or you can eliminate the both-feet bounce and just use a jogging step as a variation.

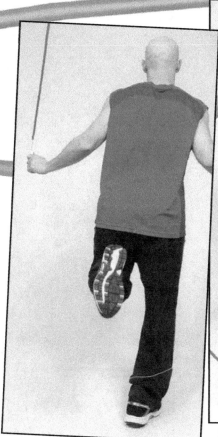

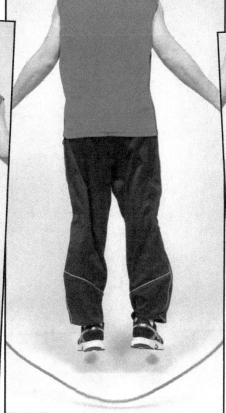

Step 1
Push off of both feet to jump the rope. Land on your right foot and bring your left heel up behind you.

Step 2
On the next turn of the rope, push off of your right foot to jump the rope and land on both feet.

Step 3
As the rope comes around this time, push off of both feet to jump the rope, land on your left foot, and bring your right heel up behind you. Continue the pattern: BF, RF, BF, LF, BF, RF, BF, LF, BF, etc.

Verbal cues: right foot   both feet   left foot

Scissors
(Intermediate)

This is a 2-Foot Jump variation, not a jogging/running step. To make this easy to remember, think, "Don't run with scissors!"

Uhhh...that's awful! Should have quit while I was ahead.

Helpful Hint:
Keep your weight centered and think more about switching legs than jumping.

Step 1
Start with the rope in back of you—left foot forward, right foot back. Tug and tap and swing the rope over your head.

Step 2
As the rope comes down, jump and switch feet (right foot forward, left foot back).

Step 3
Keep your weight centered and continue to switch your feet with every jump.

Verbal cues: | left forward, right back | right forward, left back

The Pendulum
(Intermediate)

It doesn't look like it, but this is a Jogging Step variation: left foot, right foot, left foot, right foot.

Helpful Hint:
As you push off of one foot and swing your leg in, think about transferring the energy from one leg to the other when you click your feet together. Let that energy immediately send the other leg out to the side.

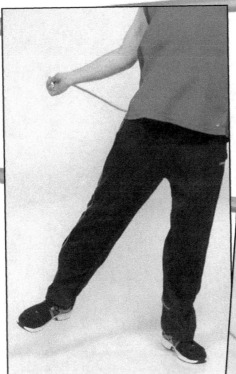

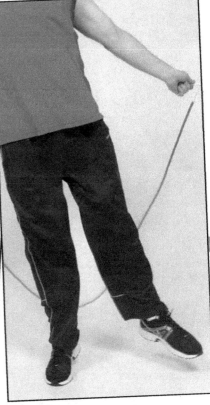

Step 1
Jump off of both feet, land on your right foot, and extend your left leg out to the side.

Step 2
Start swinging your left leg back in as you push off of your right foot to jump the rope again. As your heels click...

Step 3
Send your right leg out to the side as you land on your left foot. Repeat the alternating pattern.

Technically, this looks more like those clicking metal balls on strings, but *The Pendulum* had a better ring to it

Verbal cues:	right foot down/left foot swing	switch	left foot down/right foot swing

Knee-Ups
(Intermediate)

This is pictured as a right-foot, both-feet, left-foot, both-feet pattern. Or you can eliminate the both-feet bounce and just use a jogging step as a variation.

Helpful Hint:
Don't worry about how high you are lifting your knees. Concentrate on the footwork pattern.

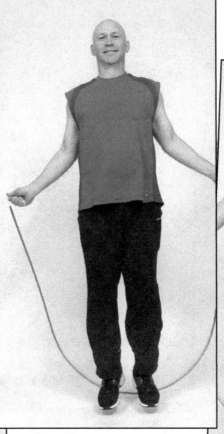

Step 1
Jump off of both feet as the rope goes under, then land on your right foot and lift your left knee.

Step 2
On the next turn of the rope, push off of your right foot, jump the rope, and land on both feet.

Step 3
Push off of both feet, land on your left foot, bring your right knee up, and continue the pattern.

Verbal cues:	right foot	both feet	left foot

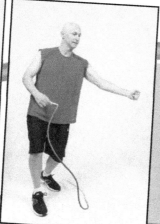

Bloopers, Stories, and Fun Facts

Funny Story:
A television crew came to film a performance of mine at a school in Clarendon Hills, IL. After the show, I stayed to sign a bunch of autographs. At the end of the line was a ten-year-old boy with a cast on his arm. He asked me if I could sign his cast, and I did. As he was walking out the door, he turned back around and, pointing to his cast, asked, "How much will this be worth when you're DEAD?"

The kids pictured in this book are not professional rope jumpers—they are normal kids, just like you, learning these tricks one by one.

I was the only professional rope jumper at the photo shoot, and I still made mistakes.

When I'm at home, I make the most mistakes when I am learning a new trick. I just keep practicing until I don't mess up as often. I only put tricks in my routine that I can do at least 95 out of 100 times without making a mistake. I practice a lot!

Catch and release moves can be tricky to do consistently, especially behind your back.

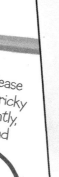

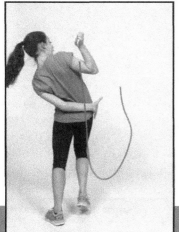

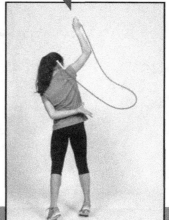

Can-Can
(Advanced)

OK, stretch out those hamstrings. It's time to kick it up a notch!

Helpful Hint:
Practice this one a lot without the rope so that you don't have to think about the pattern while you are jumping.

Step 1
Jump off of both feet and bring your right knee up as you land on your left foot.

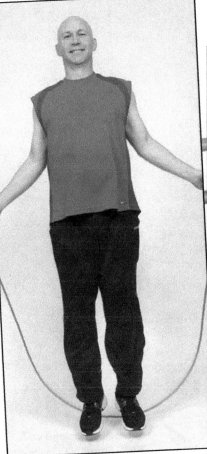

Step 2
Push off of your left foot and land on both feet.

Step 3
Jump off of both feet and kick your straight right leg out as you land on your left foot.

Verbal cues:	(both feet)	right knee	(both feet)	right kick

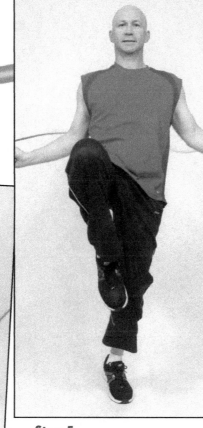

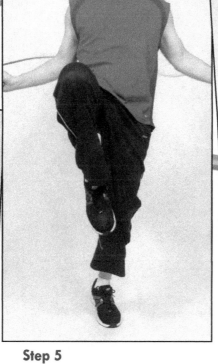

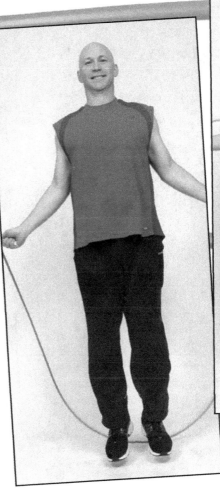

Step 4
Push off your left foot and land on both feet.

Step 5
Jump off both feet and bring your left knee up as you land on your right foot.

Step 6
Push off of your right foot and land on both feet.

Step 7
Jump off of both feet and kick your straight left leg out as you land on your right foot. Push off your right foot and continue the pattern.

| (both feet) | left knee | (both feet) | left kick |

Karaoke
(Advanced)

In my opinion, this is the hardest of the footwork skills in this book. It's a gallop step in which you alternate stepping in front and in back as you travel to the side.

Helpful Hint:
The rope only goes under on the **jogging** step. In the demonstration pictured, your right foot is jogging and your left foot is stepping.

As with all funtastic footwork tricks, practice first without the rope!

Step 1
Start with the rope behind you. As you swing it over your head, shift the weight to your left leg and lift your right foot—and get ready to move to the right.

Step 2
Push off of your left foot and jog onto your right foot as the rope goes under, then bring your left foot **in front** as you continue to move right.

Step 3
Quickly shift the weight to (by **stepping** down on) your left foot, which has crossed in front of your right foot. Begin to lift your right foot as you keep moving right.

Verbal cues: jog   step

Step 4
Push off of your left foot and jog onto your right foot as the rope goes under, then bring your left foot **in back** as you continue to move right.

Step 5
Quickly shift the weight to (by **stepping** down on) your left foot, which has crossed in back of your right foot. Begin to lift your right foot as you keep moving right.

Step 6
Push off of your left foot and jog onto your right foot as the rope goes under. Bring your left foot in front as you continue to move right.

Step 7
Quickly shift the weight to (by **stepping** down on) your left foot, which has crossed in front of your right foot. Begin to lift your right foot as you keep moving right. Repeat steps 4–7. *Variation:* Practice the Karaoke step moving to the left. Jog onto your left foot and step down with your right.

jog · step · jog · step

Crossing Skills

Here are a few crossing skills to help you get ready to do some more advanced crossing tricks.

Put both handles in your right hand and give each of these skills a try.
Don't forget to try each skill again using your left hand!

Front-Cross Side Swing
(Beginner)

You already did part of a Front-Cross Side Swing when you did a 1-Hand Figure 8 (page 27).

Helpful Hint:
Pretend that you are holding one handle in each hand. Once your arms are crossed, **keep them crossed** and keep turning your wrists to move the rope.

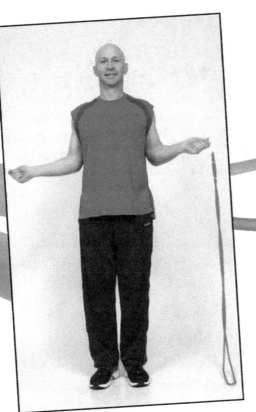

Step 1
Put both handles in your right hand and do a 1-Hand Side Swing (page 12).

Once your arms are crossed, pretend that you are scrambling eggs—one on each side.

Step 2
As the rope is above your head, begin to cross both arms in front of you.

Step 3
Cross your arms as far as you can (try to touch your elbows together if you are flexible enough) and continue turning in this crossed position.
Try it again. This time, jump to the rhythm of the rope.

Verbal cues: swing on the right   cross

Try this one hopping to the rhythm of the rope—it's tricky!

Under-the-Far-Leg Side Swing
(Intermediate)

This crossing skill is a cool trick by itself, and it will help you get ready to do the Toe! (page 76).

Helpful Hint:
Hold the ends of the handles so that you can keep the rope farther away from you.

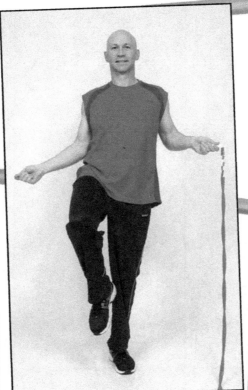

Step 1
Put both handles in your right hand and do a 1-Hand Side Swing (page 12) on your right side. Put the weight on your right foot and lift your left knee.

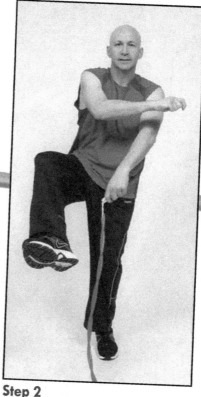

Step 2
When the rope starts to come down, begin to cross both arms in front of you (left over right) and begin to put your right hand under your left knee.

Step 3
Continue crossing your arms as far as you can and continue turning your wrists in this crossed position.

Verbal cues:	side swing	and	cross under the leg

Behind-the-Back Side Swing
(Advanced)

This one will take a little flexibility and a whole lot of practice. Don't give up!

Helpful Hint:
Again, as with most crosses, stick out the handles as far as you can.

Practice this skill while jumping to the rhythm of the rope.

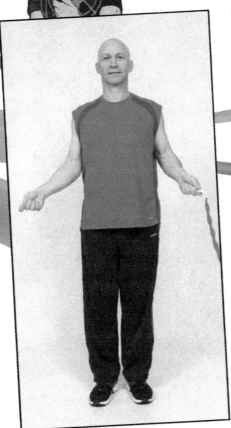

Step 1
Put both handles in your right hand and do a 1-Hand Side Swing (page 12).

Step 2
After the rope hits the ground, cross your right hand behind your back and your left hand in front.

Step 3
Continue turning in this crossed position.
Variation: Try this one with both handles in your left hand.

Verbal cues: side swing   cross behind your back

Crossing Tricks

There are many different ways to put your left hand on the right side of your body and your right hand on the left side of your body while jumping over the rope. Here are some of my favorites.

These tricks may look really complicated, but give them a try—you may surprise yourself! Can you come up with other ways to put your left hand on the right side of your body and your right hand on the left side of your body?

Backward Front Cross
(Beginner)

Believe it or not, I have found that the Backward Front Cross is the easiest one to teach. Follow all of these crossing tricks, step-by-step, and you'll be amazing your friends in no time!

Helpful Hint:
Keep your hands **low.** Hug your stomach, not your head.

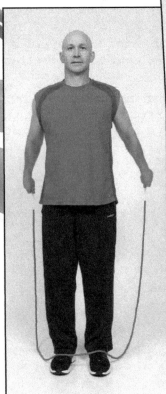

Step 1
Start with the rope in front of you, at your toes.

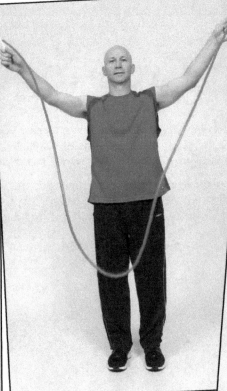

Step 2
Make a backward circle. (Bring the rope backward over your head.)

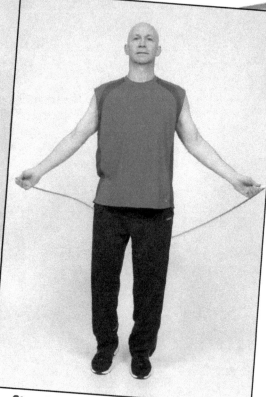

Step 3
When you feel the rope coming down toward your heels (you won't be able to see it when it's behind you), jump.

Verbal cues: backward circle

Once you cross your arms, keep them crossed.
Don't uncross your arms until you miss.

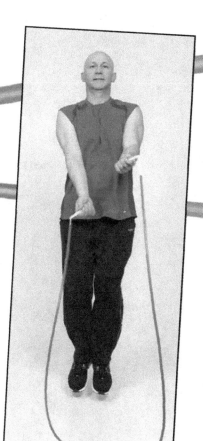

Step 4
As soon as you jump, start to cross your arms.

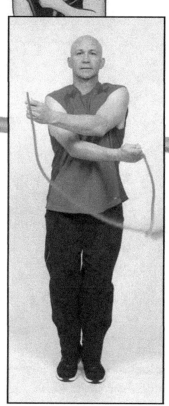

Step 5
Give your stomach a big hug—get your hands way out to the side. See if you can touch your elbows together.

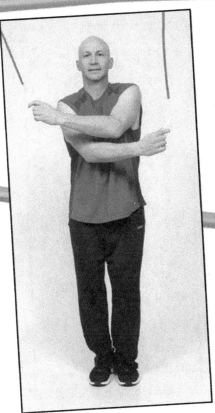

Step 6
Keep your arms crossed and continue turning the rope backward with your wrists.

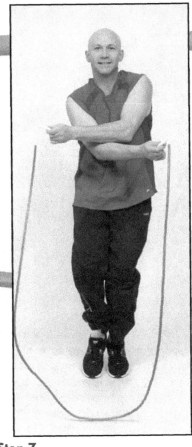

Step 7
When you feel the rope coming down toward your heels, jump. Continue jumping with your arms crossed and the rope going backward.
Variation: Once you can do a Sustained Backward Front Cross (always jumping with your arms crossed), try cross, open, cross, open with your arms.

jump and hug   keep turning   jump

The Pretzel
(Beginner)

WHAT!?! This trick is for beginners? Make sure to read the Helpful Hints safety tips first, then practice steps 1-3 over and over without the rope before you try to add the rope.

Helpful Hints:
When you are bent over, keep all the weight on your feet, not your hands—don't fall forward on your face!

Don't spend too much time with your head below your heart—if you get dizzy, stand up.

When your hands go through your legs, make sure to get your hands *way* out to the side and behind your knees so that the rope doesn't hit you in the head or face.

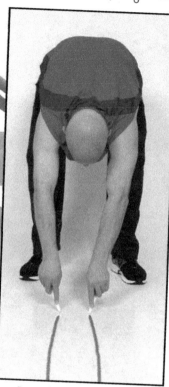
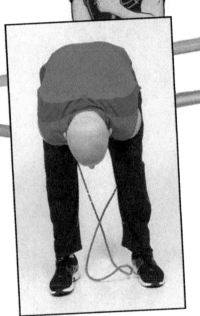
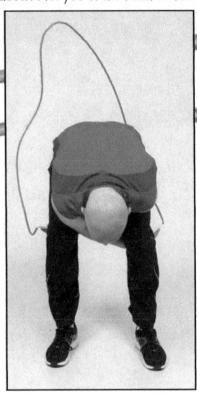

Step 1
Lay the rope on the ground in the shape of a skinny, upside-down letter **U**. Just like you were going to hike a football, bend your knees and reach forward for both handles. Keep all the weight on your feet!

Step 2
Begin to sweep your hands through your legs.

Step 3
Immediately after you sweep your hands straight through your legs, cross them so that your right hand goes behind your left knee and your left hand goes behind your right knee.

Verbal cues: upside-down letter U   football hiking stance   sweep and cross   stay down

As the rope is coming over your head, move your feet closer together, as it will be easier to jump over the rope after it hits the ground.

Don't start to stand up or jump until after the rope hits the ground.

Step 4
When the rope hits the ground, keep your hands behind your knees and jump over the rope.

Step 5
Begin to pull your hands out from behind your knees.

Step 6
Finish pulling your hands out from behind your knees as you start to stand up and bring the rope backward over your head.

Step 7
Continue turning the rope backward, over your head, and then jump.

Front Cross
(Beginner)

Here is the cross that everyone knows about. Most mistakes result from the loop being too small or from uncrossing one's arms too soon. Try it first without uncrossing your arms, like we did with the Backward Front Cross (page 62).

Helpful Hint:
Anytime you miss on a front cross, **FREEZE** and check your loop. Was it big enough to jump through? Could you stick the handles out farther? Were your feet together when you jumped?

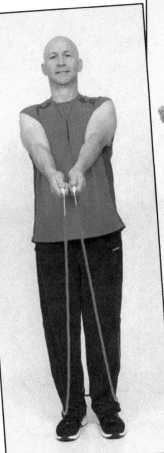

Step 1
Start with the rope at your heels, tug (bring your hands forward), and tap your fists together.

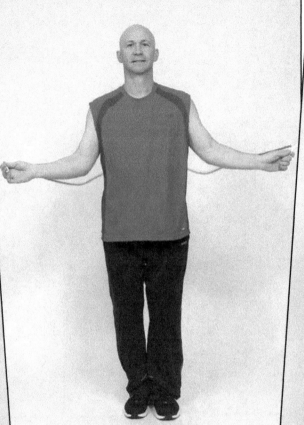

Step 2
Bring both hands down, back, and around so that the middle of the rope makes a circle all the way around you.

Step 3
When the rope is above your head, start bringing your right hand over to your left side and your left hand over to your right side.

Verbal cues: rope at heels, give a tug   make a circle

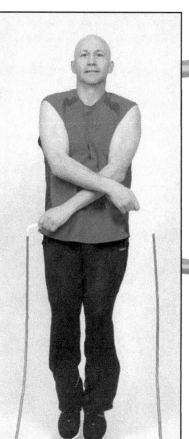

Step 4
Stick the handles out as far as you can so that the loop is as big as possible.

Step 5
Jump with your arms crossed.

Step 6
Keep turning with your arms crossed.

Step 7
As the rope clears your head, begin to uncross your arms. *Variation:* Try alternating the arm that crosses on top. Example: Jump with arms crossed right over left. Then uncross and do an open jump. Then cross left over right and jump again.

give a hug   jump   uncross

Matador Cross
(Intermediate)

This funtastic crossing trick is a lot of fun—no bull!

Helpful Hint:
Practice your 2-Hand Figure 8, leading with your left hand and your right hand, before you try a Matador Cross.

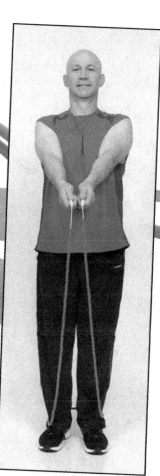

Step 1
Start with the rope at your heels, tug (bring your hands forward), and tap your fists together.

Step 2
Bring both hands down, back, and around so that the middle of the rope makes a circle all the way around you. As the rope goes over your head, start to bring your left hand over to your right side.

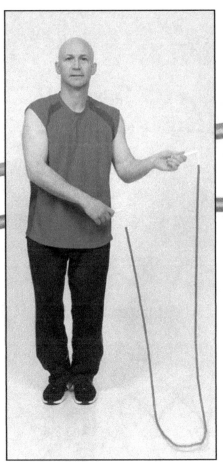

Step 3
Do an Open Side Swing (page 13) on your right side.

Verbal cues: rope at heels, give a tug   swing both on the right

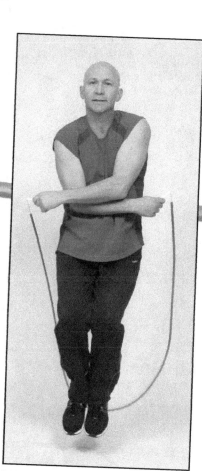

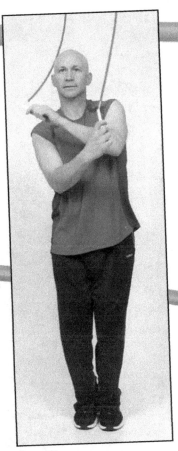

Step 4
As the rope begins to come up, leave your left hand on your right side and begin to cross all the way over with your right hand.

Step 5
Continue crossing your right hand all the way over to your left side.

Step 6
Jump with your right arm crossed on top of your left arm.

Step 7
Leave your right arm crossed and start to bring your left hand all the way to your left side.

Continued on next page.

cross with the right   jump

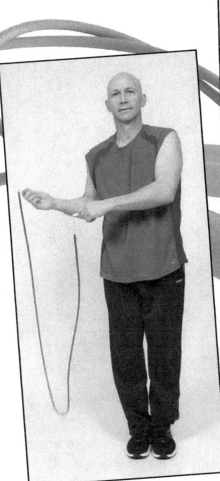

Step 8
Do an Open Side Swing (page 13) on your left side.

Step 9
As the rope begins to come up, leave your right hand on your left side and start to cross all the way over with your left hand.

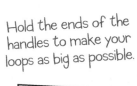

Hold the ends of the handles to make your loops as big as possible.

Step 10
Continue crossing as far as you can with your left arm crossed on top of your right arm.

Step 11
Jump with your left arm crossed over your right arm. Leave your left arm crossed and start to bring your right hand to your right side, then repeat steps 3–11.

---

swing both on the left · cross with the left · jump

Career Highlights:
The Rope Warrior has set two world records in rope jumping—for jumping rope while sitting on his BUTT!

The Rope Warrior has performed for Boris Yeltsin in Russia and for Presidents Clinton and Bush at their inaugurations.

The Rope Warrior has been on National Television over 100 times (he counts reruns), including appearances on the following:

The Today Show	EXTRA!
Good Morning America	ESPN
The NBC Nightly News	C-SPAN
Ripley's Believe It or Not!	Live! with Regis and Kathie Lee
Guinness World Records Primetime	

The Rope Warrior has performed live for over 5 million people in over 10 different countries.

Bloopers, Stories, and Fun Facts

Fun Fact:
The Rope Warrior's resting pulse has been measured as low as 27 beats per minute! (Typically, a resting heart rate is around 80 beats per minute.)

It can take a while to get the timing just right when you're working with a partner... or three.

Cannonball!

Zombie Max forgot to jump.

180 Matador
(Intermediate)

Now we're going to try turning and crossing at the same time.

Helpful Hint:
When the rope is going backward, you cross **under**.

Step 1
Start with the rope at your heels, tug (bring your hands forward), and tap your fists together.

Step 2
Bring both hands down, back, and around so that the middle of the rope makes a circle all the way around you.

Step 3
As the rope goes over your head, start to bring your right hand over to your left side and begin to turn left.

Verbal cues: side swing left

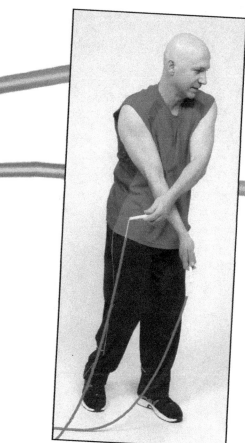

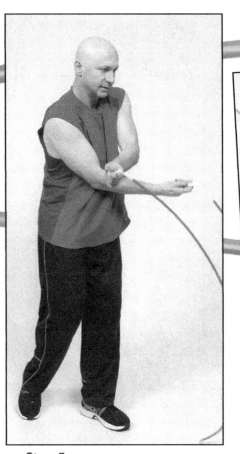

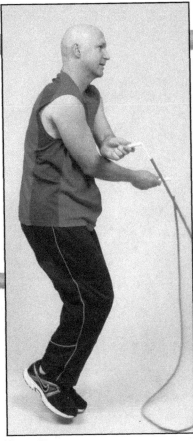

Step 4

Start to do an open side swing on your left and continue to turn left. Cross your right arm under your left arm and let your left hand go to your right side as you keep turning your body to the left.

Step 5

As you finish your 180-degree turn, you should be in a fully crossed position—with your left arm on top of your right arm and the rope going backward over your head.

Step 6

Keep turning the rope backward with your wrists and be ready to jump over the rope as it comes down by your heels.

Step 7

Jump with the rope going backward and your left arm crossed on top of your right arm. Continue jumping in this crossed position or uncross and do an open jump. *Variation:* Try to side swing right, turn right, and cross under with your left hand.

Double Crosser
(Advanced)

Don't try this one until you can do a Front Cross (page 66) with a cross-open-cross-open pattern, alternating your top hand without missing.

Helpful Hint:
If you are better at crossing one hand on top than the other, start with your weak hand on top and switch-cross to your strong hand.

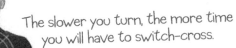

The slower you turn, the more time you will have to switch-cross.

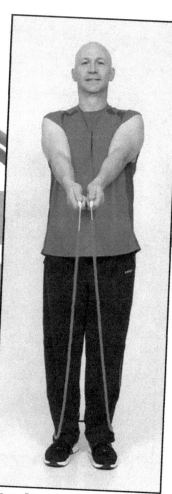

Step 1
Start with the rope at your heels, tug (bring your hands forward), and tap your fists together.

Step 2
Bring both hands down, back, and around so that the middle of the rope makes a circle all the way around you. When the rope is above your head, start crossing your arms (with your left arm crossing on top of your right arm).

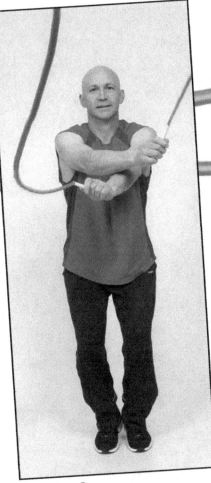

Step 3
Stick the handles out as far as you can so that the loop is as big as possible.

Also, don't pull your arms too far apart after your first cross. Just uncross a little and immediately recross as far as you can.

Step 4
Jump with your arms crossed (left over right).

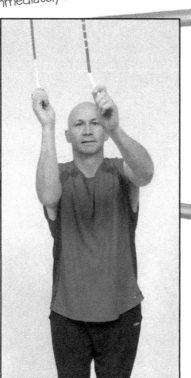

Step 5
When the rope is above your head, uncross your arms and then immediately begin to recross them with your right arm on top of your left arm this time.

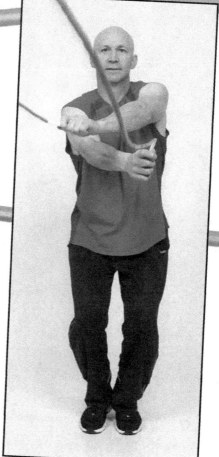

Step 6
Cross your arms as far as you can, with your right arm crossed over your left arm.

Step 7
Jump with your right arm crossed over your left arm.

The Toe
(Advanced)

Remember the Under-the-Far-Leg Side Swing skill you did last chapter (page 59)? Here is why we practiced it.

Helpful Hint:
Just see if you can get the rope into a good crossing position first without jumping. Do steps 1–3 and let the rope hit your right foot instead of jumping over it.

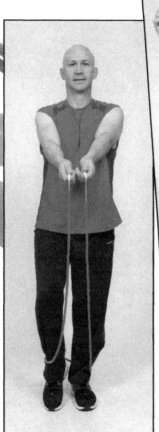

Step 1
Shift weight to your right foot. Tug, tap, and begin to swing the rope over your head.

Step 2
Put all of your weight on your right foot, lift your left knee, and as the rope is above your head, begin to cross both arms in front of you, left over right.

Step 3
Continue crossing and put your right hand under your left knee. Cross as far as you can and continue turning your wrists in this crossed position.

Verbal cues: circle   hug

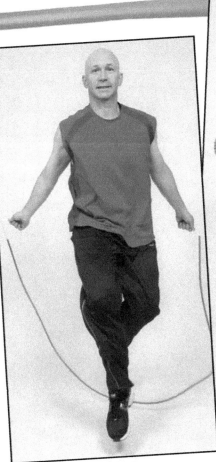

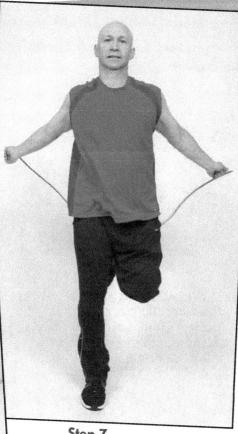

Step 4
With your left arm crossed on top of your right arm and your right hand under your left knee, hop on your right foot.

Step 5
Keep turning and hopping in this crossed position. When you are ready to get out of it, do steps 6–7.

Step 6
After you hop, begin to uncross and let the rope go past your left foot. Then immediately jog onto your left foot as you finish uncrossing, and then pick up your right foot in back of you.

Step 7
Say, "Ta-Daaah!"

Some jumpers call this trick "The Toad." It could be that I just misheard it the first time.

hop   uncross

Handcuffed
(Advanced)

Everyone should give this funtastic crossing trick a try, although flexible people may have a little easier time with it.

Helpful Hint:
Practice without swinging the rope. Start with one handle in each hand and the middle of the rope on the ground in front of you. As you jump over the rope, bring your hands behind you and then cross them as far as possible behind your back.

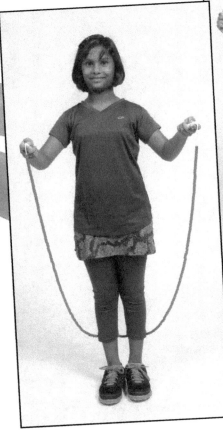

Step 1
Start with the rope at your heels.

Step 2
Swing the rope over your head and then do one open jump.

Step 3
As soon as you jump over the rope, bring your hands behind you and begin to cross them behind your back.

Verbal cues: jump over   cross behind

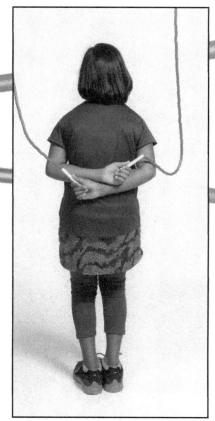

Step 4
Stick the handles out as far to the side as possible.

Step 5
Keep turning your wrists forward, with your hands crossed as far as possible behind your back.

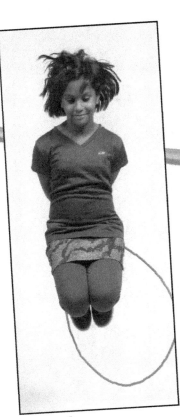

Step 6
Jump over the rope.

Step 7
Uncross and continue jumping with the rope going forward.

jump over   uncross, jump

Gentleman's Cross
(Advanced)

Practice this funtastic trick and you'll be able to say, "I can do a crisscross with one hand tied behind my back!"

Helpful Hint:
Practice steps 1–4 without jumping so that you can get the loop to come over your head in a good position.

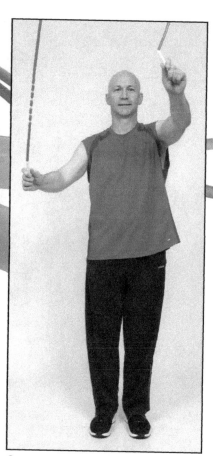

Step 1
Swing the rope over your head and start to bring your right hand over to your left side.

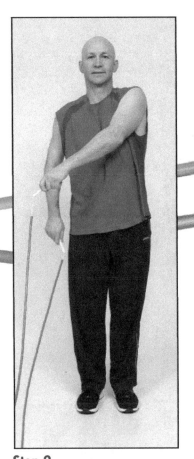

Step 2
Swing both hands on the left. (Do it more like you are paddling a canoe than doing an open side swing. Your left hand gets there first and stays close to your body.)

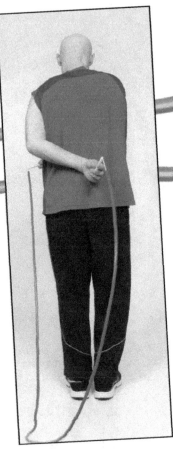

Step 3
As the rope swings on the left and your right hand gets to your left side, get your left hand behind your back and as far to the right as possible.

Verbal cues: swing on the left   left hand behind

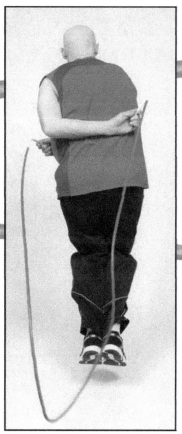

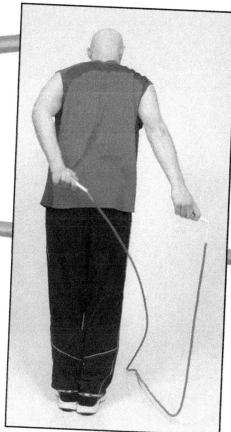

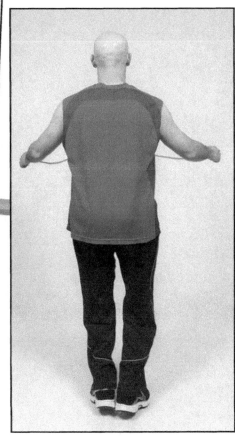

Step 4
Keep your right hand crossed in front and your left hand crossed in back, and let the rope go over your head.

Step 5
Keep turning with your wrists in this crossed position and continue jumping.

You might have to angle your body a little to jump through the loop.

Step 6
When you are ready to get out of this crossed position, let the rope go above your head and then let your right hand start to uncross and follow the rope to your right side.

Step 7
Uncross your arms and do an open jump. *Variation:* Try putting your right hand behind your back. Swing on the right and cross your right hand behind your back.

Miscellaneous Skills

Here are a few skills that will help you get ready for the Cat's Cradle, the Leg-Up Figure 8, and the Leg Up found in the next chapter.

The Stall
(Beginner)

You need to know this skill to do The Cat's Cradle, but it is also another way to change the direction of the rope.

Helpful Hint:
The rope only goes over your head **one** time during this skill.

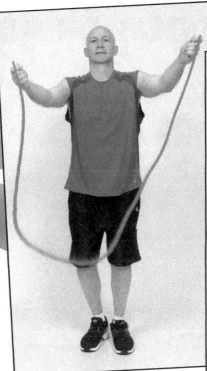

Step 1
Start with the rope in front of you and make a backward circle.

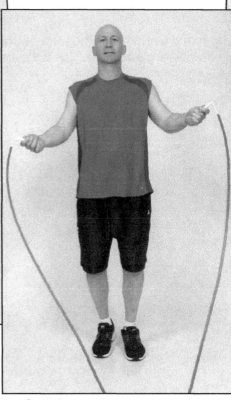

Step 2
Jump over the rope as it comes down toward your heels.

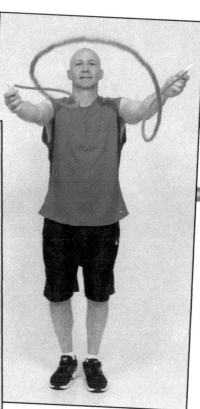

Step 3
Immediately stop/stall the rope in front of you so that it does not go over your head again.

1-Handed Figure 8 Under the Leg
(Intermediate)

You need to practice this skill for a Leg-Up Figure 8.

Helpful Hint:
In step 3, you may have to bring your left foot to the right and angle it.

Step 1
Start with a 1-Hand Side Swing on your right side, put your weight on your right foot, and lift your left knee. As the rope comes down, cross your right hand under your left knee so that the rope swings on your left side.

Step 2
As the rope swings on your left side with your right hand under your left knee, angle your left leg so that the next swing can go back to your right again.

Step 3
As the rope comes down, bring your right hand back to your right side and swing on the right. *Variation:* Put both handles in your left hand and do a figure 8 under your right leg.

1-Handed, Leg-Up Side Swing
(Intermediate)

This skill will help you with the Leg Up (or with your flamingo training 😊).

Helpful Hint:
Try to get your right elbow all the way under your right knee, if possible.

As you do step 1, see if you can hop on your left foot.

Step 1
Start with a right-hand side swing. When the rope is up, lift your right knee and start to put your right hand on the inside and then under your right knee. As the rope hits the floor, stick your right hand out as far as possible. Continue turning the rope with your wrists.

Step 2
To get out, when the rope is up, angle your right foot to the left and start to go from a 1-handed side swing on the **right** to a 1-handed crossed side swing on the **left**.

Step 3
Finish the 1-handed crossed side swing on the left side as you put your right foot down. *Variation:* Try it with your left hand all the way under your left knee.

Verbal cues:	side swing right	leg up	angle foot	side swing left

Miscellaneous Tricks

These tricks don't fit nicely into a specific category,
but they are *funtastic*!

This chapter is loaded with some of my favorite tricks.
Try some turns, releases, leg-ups, and more.

Back-Foot Catch Reverse
(Beginner)

Here is a funtastic way to reverse the direction of the rope.

Helpful Hint:
Only lift your back heel—keep the ball of your foot on the ground. Also, keep your weight centered—don't lean forward too much when you kick the rope over.

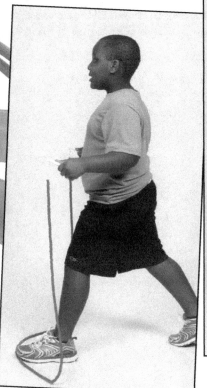

Step 1
Start with one handle in each hand and the middle of the rope at your toes. Slide your right foot back and lift your right **heel**.

Step 2
Make a backward circle (don't jump) and catch the rope underneath your right foot. Tug slightly to remove the slack.

Step 3
Keep the tension on the rope and lift/kick your right foot back/up to send the rope forward, over your head.

Verbal cues: rope at toes   right foot back   backward circle   catch   kick

Bowling
(Beginner)

This is a great trick to do with young jumpers or non-jumpers. Just watch out for flying handles!

Helpful Hint:
Keep your arm and the rope **behind** you as you start the trick, and then walk forward.

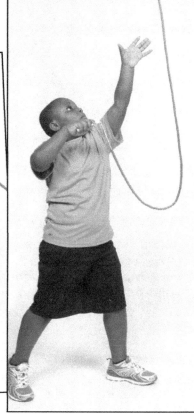

Step 1
Start walking forward, dragging the full straight rope behind you. (You can pretend that you're walking/dragging behind you a big dog that doesn't want to go for a walk.)

Step 2
With an underhand "bowling" motion, push the rope out in front of you.

Step 3
Catch the handle.
Challenge: Try to jump right over the loop when you catch the handle, and then continue jumping forward.

Verbal cues: walk the heavy dog   bowl   catch

YEE HA!
(Beginner)

This funtastic 1-handed trick is part step-through and part cowboy rodeo roping trick.

Helpful Hint:
Try to turn slowly and keep your legs straight.

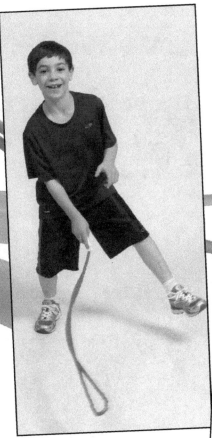

Step 1
Start with both handles in your left hand. Swing the rope sideways (clockwise as you look down,) toward your right leg. Start to lift your right leg to the side.

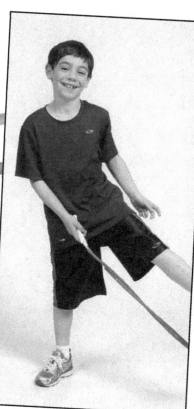

Step 2
Keep a straight right leg, continue to lift your leg to the side, and step over the rope.

Step 3
Keep spinning the rope clockwise below you. Swing the rope between your legs and step out with a straight left leg.
Variation: put both handles in your right hand, turn the rope counter-clockwise and lift your left leg first.

Verbal Cues: step over   step out

Fishing
(Beginner)

Here is a funtastic trick to start a routine. We'll show you basic Fishing first and then add some variations.

Helpful Hint:
Keep a straight arm when you "lift." If you minimize and slow your arm movement, you will have more control.

Step 1
Start with the rope stretched out in a straight line in front of you and hold one handle in your right hand. Back away from the rope as much as you can.

Step 2
Keep your right arm straight and lift it up. (Do it softly the first time.)

Step 3
Catch the handle with your left hand.

Continued on next page.

Verbal cues: straight rope   straight right arm   lift   catch

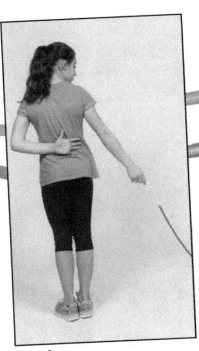

Step 4

Funtastic Fishing Challenge: Can you add a jump? Repeat steps 1 and 2 from Fishing. Immediately after you lift your right arm, step back and to the right as you drop your right arm down. This should get the loop in a good position to jump through. Bend your knees and catch the handle in your left hand.

Step 5

Let the middle of the rope fall in front of you, and then jump over it. Continue jumping forward.

Step 6

Funtastic Fishing Challenge II: Can you "Fish" behind your back? Instead of facing the rope, turn sideways and put your left hand **behind your back.** Angle your body so that you give yourself a good chance to catch the rope with your left hand.

Step 7

Lift your straight right arm so that the handle on the ground will go behind your back.

step back   jump   sideways   lift

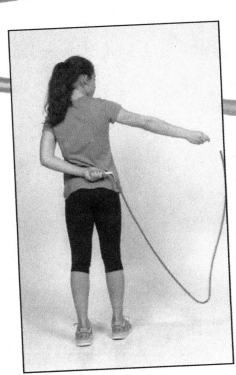

Step 9
Let the loop swing behind you as your left arm uncrosses, and then begin to swing the rope forward over your head.

Step 8
Catch the handle behind your back with your left hand.

Step 10
As the rope comes over your head, bend your knees and prepare to jump.

Step 11
Continue jumping with the rope going forward.

180
Jedi Turn
(Beginner)

Originally, this was the mistake everyone makes when trying to do a 180 Backward to Forward (page 98). No problem—now it is one of my favorite funtastic tricks to teach!

Helpful Hint:
First, practice steps 1 and 2. Then practice step 3 only. Then try steps 3–7.

Step 1
Face the side. Put one handle in each hand and put the middle of the rope at your toes.

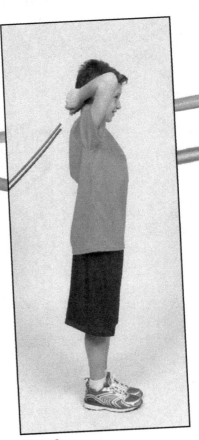

Step 2
Softly pick up the rope (because it is going to hit you this time) and put your fists together, behind your head.

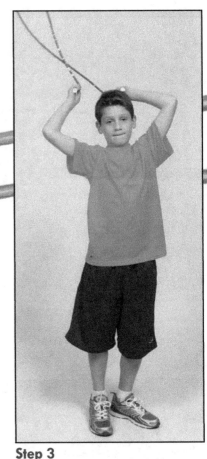

Step 3
Repeat steps 1 and 2. But instead of letting the rope hit you, turn and face the front so that the rope swings behind you.

Verbal cues: rope at toes   pick it up   turn   hands behind

Step 4
Continue to turn.

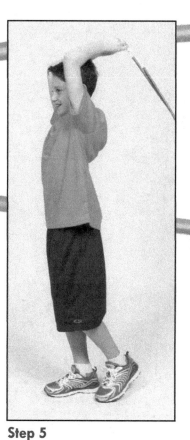

Step 5
Continue to turn your body so that you face the **opposite**-side wall as the rope comes forward over your head. Start to open up your hands and be ready to jump.

Step 6
Jump over the rope with the rope going forward. (You are now facing the opposite wall.)

Step 7
Continue jumping.

swing it over   turn   jump

180 Forward to Backward
(Beginner)

Here is another way to go from forward jumping to backward jumping. Instead of changing the direction of the rope, you change the direction in which you are facing.

Helpful Hint:
First practice steps 1–5 without jumping. Just let the rope go backward over your head, and let it hit your heels instead of jumping over it.

Step 1
Start with one handle in each hand and the middle of the rope at your heels. Tug and tap.

Step 2
Swing the rope over your head.

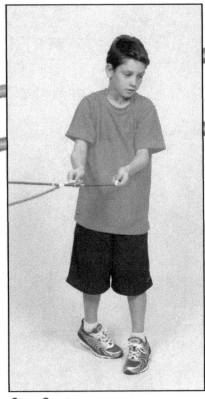

Step 3
As the rope comes over your head, start bringing your left hand over to your right side and start turning your body to the right.

Verbal cues: heels, tug, tap   circle   side swing right

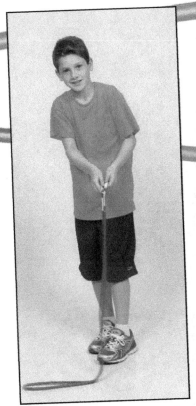

Step 4
Side swing on the right and keep turning your body. Follow the rope.

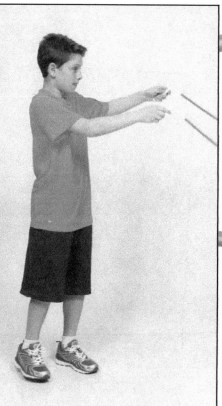

Step 5
As you finish turning 180 degrees, start to bring the rope backward over your head.

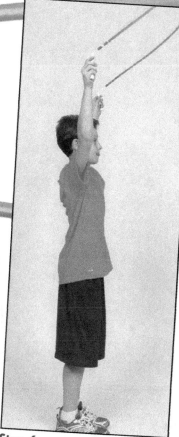

Step 6
As the rope goes backward over your head, start to bend your knees and prepare to jump.

Step 7
Continue jumping backward.

180 Backward to Forward
(Beginner)

Here is another way in which you can go from jumping backward to jumping forward.

Helpful Hint:
Try starting with the rope at your toes and do steps 3–6. Then go back and add the backward jump (steps 1 and 2) to the beginning of the trick.

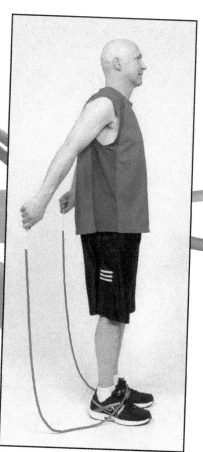

Step 1
Start with one handle in each hand and the middle of the rope at your toes.

Step 2
Swing the rope backward over your head and do one backward jump.

Step 3
As soon as you land, pick up the middle of the rope and start turning to the left.

Step 4
Keep the middle of the rope above your head (but not behind it) and keep turning to the left.

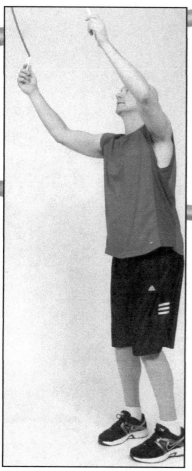

Step 5
Finish your 180-degree turn and begin to bring the middle of the rope down toward your toes.

Step 6
Continue to bring the middle of the rope down toward your toes, and prepare to jump.

Step 7
Jump with the rope going forward.

turn

forward jump

360 Turn
(Intermediate)

Now we combine parts of the two 180-degree turns to do a 360.

Helpful Hint:
Think about bouncing the middle of the rope off of the floor. As soon as it hits, lift it up and continue turning.

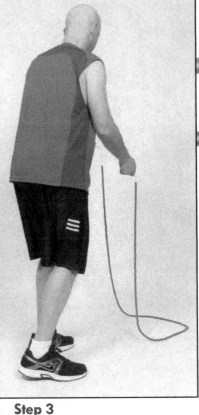

Step 1
Start with one handle in each hand and the middle of the rope at your heels. Tug, tap, and swing the rope over your head. As the rope comes over your head, start bringing your left hand over to your right side.

Step 2
Keep turning to the right as the rope hits the ground.

Step 3
Keep turning to the right, get ready to pick up the rope, and continue turning to the right.

Verbal cues: heels, tug, tap   circle   swing right   turn right

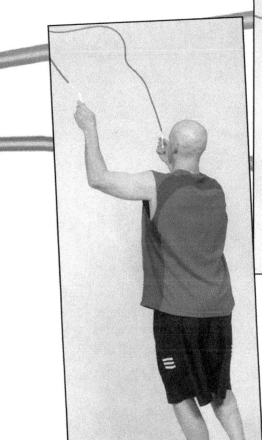

Step 4
Pick up the middle of the rope (but keep it in front of you) and continue turning all the way around.

Step 5
Keep turning to the right. The middle of the rope can go **above** your head but not **behind** it.

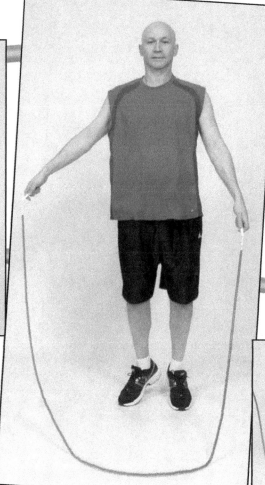

Step 6
Finish the 360-degree turn as you pull the middle of the rope down toward your toes.

Step 7
Jump forward over the rope. *Advanced 360:* Once you practice the 360 a lot, try to do the whole trick in the air with a big 360-degree jump.

lift it up   turn all the way around   jump

Cat's Cradle
(Intermediate)

This is one of my favorite funtastic tricks to teach. It looks tricky, but hang in there and don't give up!

Helpful Hint:
The rope will go over your head only **one** time during this trick (in step 2). Practice The Stall (page 84).

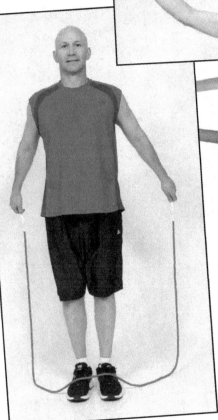

Step 1
Start with the rope in front of you and the middle of the rope on top of your feet.

Step 2
Make a backward circle over your head.

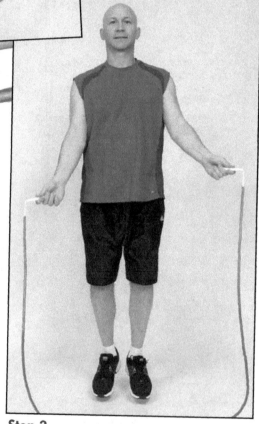

Step 3
Jump. As your feet are leaving the floor, be ready to clap your fists together.

Verbal cues: backward circle   jump

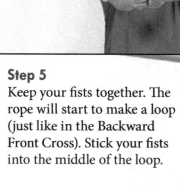

Step 5
Keep your fists together. The rope will start to make a loop (just like in the Backward Front Cross). Stick your fists into the middle of the loop.

Step 7
Cat's Cradle!

Step 4
Immediately after you jump, clap your fists together. One fist should be a little higher than the other.

Step 6
Let the loop land on your forearms and start to pull your hands apart to reveal...

clap   catch

Leg-Up Figure 8
(Intermediate)

This crazy-looking trick is just a 2-Hand Figure 8 with a left-hand lead. You just add the Leg Up to make it look fancier.

Helpful Hint:
Let your left hand do nearly all the work to angle the loop around your left foot.

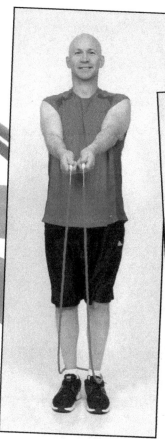

Step 1
Start with the rope behind you. Tug and tap.

Step 2
Shift some weight to your right leg and be ready to lift your left knee.

Step 3
Swing the rope over your head and lift your left knee.

Verbal cues: heels, tug, tap   circle

Step 4
Start bringing your right hand over to the left.

Step 5
Your left foot goes inside the loop as you do an Open Side Swing (page 13) on your left.

Step 6
As the loop comes around, start to bring both hands to the right side and get your left hand going all the way to the right. Angle your left foot so that it does not get caught on the way out of the loop.

Your left hand is now all the way on your right side as you do a Crossed Side Swing (page 14) on the right.

Step 7
Finish the Crossed Side Swing on the right, then open your arms and continue jumping with the rope going forward.

swing on the left   swing on the right

Leg Up
(Intermediate)

No matter how many super-advanced tricks I put in my routine, this intermediate trick always gets the biggest reaction from the audience.

Helpful Hint:
Hold the end of the handle so that it will stick out more.

Step 1
Start with the rope in back. Put your weight on your left foot, tug, and tap.

Step 2
Swing the rope over your head and be ready to lift your right knee up and out to the side.

Step 3
As the rope comes down, bring your right hand and then your right elbow (if you are flexible enough) to the inside of and then under your right knee. Let the rope hit your left leg. (We are just getting into position, and we'll jump on the next try.)

Verbal cues: heels, tug, tap   circle   leg up

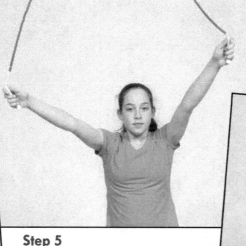

Step 5
Swing the rope over your head and be ready to lift your right knee up and out to the side.

Try to keep good posture during this trick. If you don't stay upright, I have a hunch you'll be hunching. 🙂

Step 4
Start with the rope in back. Put your weight on your left foot. Tug and tap.

Step 6
As the rope comes down, bring your right hand and then your right elbow (if you are flexible enough) to the inside of and then under your right knee. Then HOP on your left leg.

Step 7
Continue hopping and smiling. (The crowd LOVES this trick.) When you have milked it for all it's worth, here is how to get out: As the rope comes over, start to slide your right hand to the left. Angle your right foot so it does not get caught on the way out, and do an **open** side swing on the left as you put your right foot down. *Variation:* To start this trick already in the leg-up position, start with the rope in front. Step over with your left foot. Lift your right knee and put your right hand on the inside and all the way under your right leg. Tug and tap, circle and hop.

heels, tug, tap   circle   leg up and hop

Side Leg Lift
(Intermediate)

This is another funtastic trick that will require a lot of practice. Make sure to follow the steps carefully!

Helpful Hint:
Make sure to keep your leg straight and your foot flexed in step 5. Keep the rope taught and use your **leg** to move the rope.

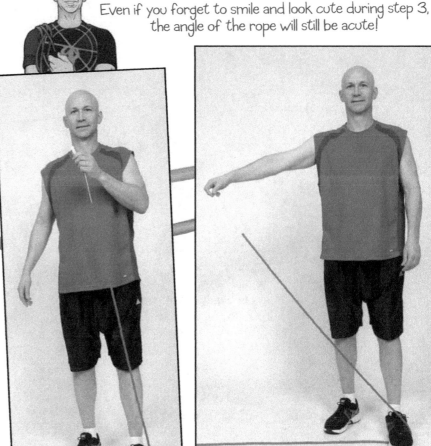

Even if you forget to smile and look cute during step 3, the angle of the rope will still be acute!

Step 1
Hold the rope in front of you and step on the middle of the rope with the middle of your right foot.

Step 2
Drop the rope out of your left hand, then slide your right foot to the right so that the part of the rope on the ground is straight.

Step 3
Switch the handle that is in your right hand to your left hand. Keep the rope pinned under your right foot.

Verbal cues:	step	drop and straighten	switch hands

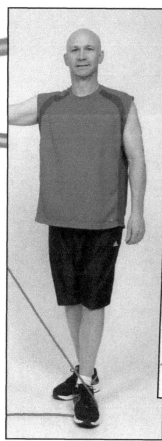

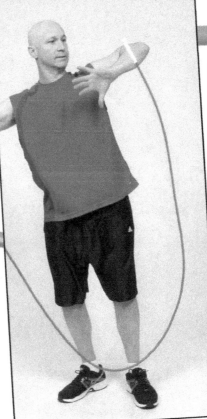

Step 4
Place your left foot behind your right foot. Keep the weight on your left foot and the tension on the rope.

Step 5
Keep the rope taught between your left hand and right foot. Sweep your **straight** right leg to the right.

Step 6
Keep the tension on the rope with your left hand. Get ready to catch the handle with your right hand.

Step 7
As you catch the handle in your right hand, start to turn your body to the left.

Continued on next page.

left foot behind   sweep your right leg   catch   turn

Step 8
Continue to turn to your left and begin to bring the rope backward over your head. Keep your hands open. (Don't cross them.)

Step 9
Get ready to do a jump with the rope going backward.

Step 10
Jump.

Step 11
Continue jumping with the rope going backward.

Diagonal Release
(Advanced)

Here is another trick that comes from rhythmic gymnastics. You may need a little more space and ceiling height.

Helpful Hint:
Before you begin, pick out a spot on the wall you are facing and aim your handle release at maybe three-quarters of the way up the wall and then a bit to the left. (Adjust as necessary.)

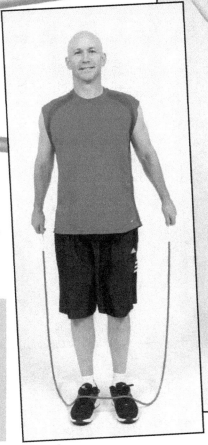

Step 1
Start with the middle of the rope on the top of your feet. Bring your hands back so that you can make a nice, big circle.

Step 2
Start to make a big, slow backward circle.

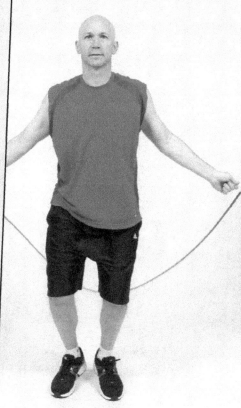

Step 3
Begin to speed up the rope as it comes down toward your heels.

Continued on next page.

Verbal cues: big backward circle

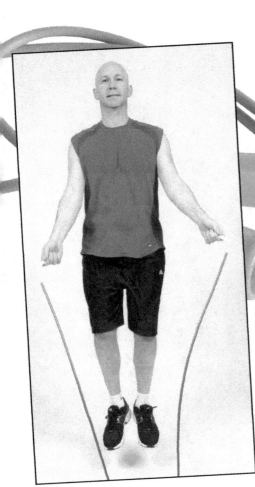

Step 4
Do a backward jump over the rope.

Step 5
Bring your hands and straight arms up to the diagonal.

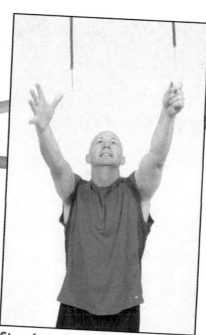

Step 6
Release the handle from your left hand and let it fly toward the spot you picked out on the wall. (See Helpful Hints.)

Step 7
Leave your arms in a diagonal position as the rope flips around.

If you want to release with your right hand, pick a spot on the wall that is three-quarters of the way up and a bit to the right.

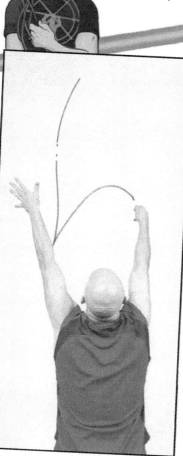

Step 8
Keep your arms in a diagonal position but begin to spread them apart.

Step 9
Catch the handle in your left hand as you bend your knees and prepare to jump.

Step 10
Jump over the loop with the rope going forward.

Step 11
Continue jumping with the rope going forward.

catch   jump

Partner Jumping Skills

Here are some beginner skills where two partners work together with one rope.

All of these skills are for non-jumpers to try, so find a partner, and a single rope that is at least one size bigger than your individual rope (see rope-sizing chart on page 2). With a little practice, teamwork, and communication, you will be ready to try some of the funtastic partner jumping tricks in the next chapter.

Under-the-Leg Pass
(Beginner)

This one is just like
1, 2, 3 Under (page 16).

Helpful Hint:
If the rope is turning **clockwise**, hold the rope in your **right** hand. If the rope is turning **counterclockwise**, hold the rope in your **left** hand.

Step 1
Stand face-to-face with your partner and hold one handle each. Begin to turn the rope. Make sure that the rope is in the correct hand (see Helpful Hints) and the middle of the rope hits the ground with each swing. Pass the rope from one hand to the other, under your leg. (I suggest right hand under left leg or left hand under right leg.)

Step 2
Begin to lower your leg as you prepare to pass the handle again.

Have one partner at a time switch under the leg.

Step 3
Return the handle to your original hand.

Double Yo-Yo
(Beginner)

Here is a funtastic skill that will make you dizzy!

Helpful Hint:

Here's a safety tip: Make sure to wrap the rope around your waist. Do not wrap the rope around your neck, feet, or legs.

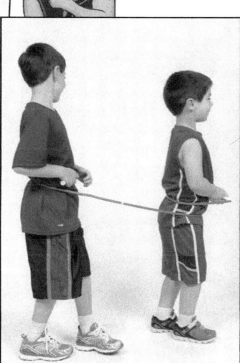

It's just like being a human yo-yo, without the ups and downs. 😊

Step 1
Each partner holds one handle, places it at his or her belly button, and stands far away from the other partner. Both partners begin to slowly spin around in a circle. The rope will start wrapping around their waist.

Step 2
Then they lightly bump in the middle.

Step 3
Both partners slowly spin in the opposite direction to unwrap the rope.

Verbal cues: handles at belly buttons   slowly spin   lightly bump   spin back out

Jump to the Middle
(Beginner)

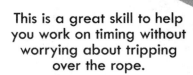

This is a great skill to help you work on timing without worrying about tripping over the rope.

Helpful Hint:
Make sure that you are up in the air each time the rope hits the ground. Always stay facing your partner.

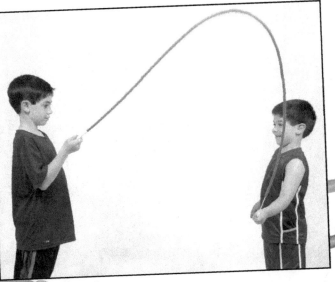

Step 1
Stand face-to-face with your partner and hold one handle each. Begin to turn the rope. Make sure that the rope is in the correct hand (see Helpful Hints on page 116) and the middle of the rope hits the ground with each swing.

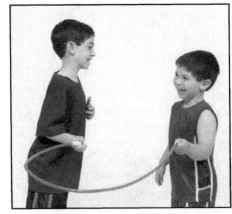

Step 3
Stay facing your partner, continue jumping, and then jump backward, away from your partner.
Variations: Try jogging, skipping, hopping, galloping, walking, and sliding.

Step 2
Begin to jump toward your partner, to the rhythm of the rope.

Verbal cues: jump to the middle   jump back out

Cool Jump-Rope Tricks You Can Do

One Turns
(Beginner)

Can you turn your body
and turn the rope at
the same time?

Helpful Hint:
Make sure to put your hand
behind your head when you turn
your body. If it feels awkward
turning in one direction, try
changing the direction in
which you turn your body,
or try changing the direction
of the rope.

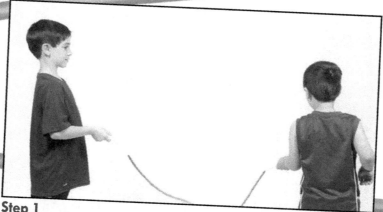

Step 1
Stand face-to-face with your partner and hold one handle each.
Begin to turn the rope. Make sure that the rope is in the correct
hand (see Helpful Hints on page 116) and the middle of the rope
hits the ground with each swing. One partner begins to turn
around in a circle.

Give each partner a
turn to turn!

Step 3
Continue turning in that
same direction until you
are back to your starting
position.

Step 2
Put your hand behind your head
when your back is to your partner.

As the Worm Turns
(Beginner)

Here is a funtastic partner trick that will strengthen your abdominal and lower back muscles—and help dust the floor!

Helpful Hint:
Slowly go down to the floor. Don't drop down to a hard floor too quickly.

Step 1
Stand face-to-face with your partner and hold one handle each. Begin to turn the rope. Make sure that the rope is in the correct hand (see Helpful Hints on page 116) and the middle of the rope hits the ground with each swing.

Step 2
Partner 1 begins to slowly go down to the ground... first one knee...

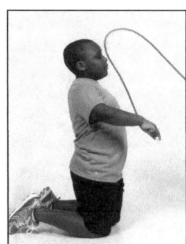

Step 3
Then the other knee.

| Verbal cues: | face-to-face | turn the rope | knee | other knee |

Step 4
Then a hand…

Step 5
Partner 1 goes all the way down to his or her stomach.

Step 6
Both partners continue to turn the rope, then partner 1 slowly stands back up.

Step 7
Partner 2 slowly goes down to the ground.

The Bullfighter
(Beginner)

This skill doesn't specifically prepare you for any of next chapter's tricks. It's just a lot of fun!

Helpful Hint:
Make sure that the loop is as big as possible and that the middle of the rope is touching the ground. If you are the bull, don't charge at full speed!

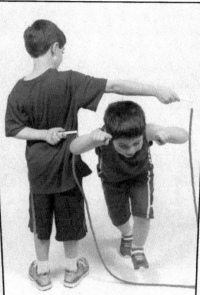

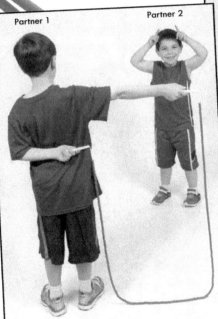

Partner 1   Partner 2

Step 1
Partner 1 will be the matador, and partner 2 will be the bull. Partner 1 holds one handle in each hand and puts the rope behind himself or herself. Partner 1 puts his or her right arm straight out and puts his or her left arm behind the back as far as it will go.

Step 2
Partner 2 **slowly** charges through the loop and then turns around toward partner 1 again.

Step 3
Partner 1 switches arms so that the left arm is now straight out and the right arm is behind the back. Partner 2 charges through again. Partner 1 continues switching arms, and partner 2 continues charging.

Question: How do you stop a bull from charging? Answer: Take away its credit card!

Verbal cues: one arm straight out   the other arm behind your back   switch to the other side

Step Over
(Beginner)

One partner powers the rope while the other partner does a 360 around the handle. Don't worry, it sounds more complicated than it is.

Helpful Hint:
Make sure that you are spinning the rope in the correct direction. If the rope is in your right hand, step over with your left foot first. If the rope is in your left hand, step over with your right foot first.

Partner 2

Partner 1

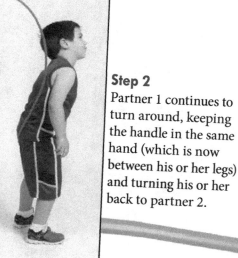

Step 2
Partner 1 continues to turn around, keeping the handle in the same hand (which is now between his or her legs) and turning his or her back to partner 2.

Step 1
Stand face-to-face with your partner and each hold one handle. Begin to turn the rope. Make sure that the rope is in the correct hand (see Helpful Hints on page 116) and the middle of the rope hits the ground with each swing. Partner 1 holds his or her turning hand low and begins to step over the rope with the opposite foot.

Step 3
Partner 1 continues to go around the handle and steps out of the rope. Continue turning the rope and let partner 2 step over.
Challenge: If at least one of the partners can jump rope by himself or herself, try having one partner jumping inside the rope while the other partner does a step-over.

Partner Mousetrap
(Beginner)

This is just like the Mousetrap (page 10), except that each partner holds one handle.

Helpful Hint:
Communicate with your partner so that you both start at the same time.

Step 1
Each partner holds one handle of the same rope. Partner 1 starts with the middle of the rope at his or her heels, and partner 2 faces partner 1's side.

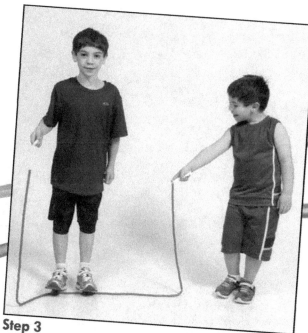

Step 3
As the rope comes down, partner 1 lifts his or her toes and traps the rope under his or her feet. Then partner 1 lifts his or her heels, and both partners swing the rope around again. Repeat step 3.
Challenge: Can you both stand side by side, handles in your outside hands, and Mousetrap together?

Step 2
The partners say, "Ready, set, go," and on "go," they swing the rope forward, over partner 1's head.

Verbal cues: heels circle trap release

High Five
(Beginner)

Here is a great skill for learning to turn the rope **slowly**.

Helpful Hint:
Turn the rope slowly and move in close together before you try to do a high five.

Step 1
Stand face-to-face with your partner and hold one handle each. Begin to turn the rope. Turn the rope as slowly as possible. Both partners count, "1, 2, 3," as the rope passes their non-turning hand. (If they both have their handle in the correct hand, their non-turning hand will be on the same side as they stand face-to-face.)

Step 2
On the next turn of the rope, both partners say, "High five!" as the rope passes their non-turning hand and they lean in and high five each other.

Step 3
Immediately after the high five, both partners back away from each other and continue turning the rope between them. Repeat steps 2 and 3.

Verbal cues: each hold one handle   turn slowly   1, 2, 3, high five   and out

The Felix Helix

(Beginner)

This trick is named after our oldest son, Felix, who is pictured here with our youngest son, Max. When one half of the rope is up, the other half of the rope is down.

Helpful Hint:
Let partner 1 get the rope started while partner 2 holds his or her turning hand still.

Step 1
The partners face each other, and each partner holds one handle of the rope. Don't start turning yet!

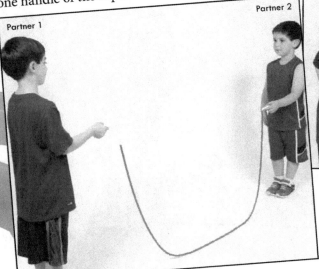

Partner 1

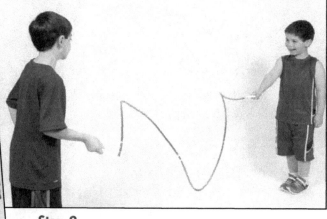

Partner 2

Step 2
Partner 1 starts making small, fast circles with the rope. Partner 2 holds his or her hand still and does not turn. You may see two, three, four, or more small waves in the rope.

Step 3
Partner 1 gradually makes slower, larger circles until one half of the rope is up while the other half is down. Partner 2 can now join in the turning.

Verbal cues: quick, small circles   let the circles get bigger

Partner Jumping Tricks

Here are just a few of my favorite partner jumping tricks for two people using one rope.

Consider these tricks as a little sneak preview of the dozens of partner
tricks that will be in the next funtastic book of skills and tricks!

Helicopter
(Beginner)

Here is a real funtasic partner jumping trick. Make sure that you are not too close to anyone else before you swing the rope around.

Helpful Hint:
The partner swinging the rope around should watch his or her partner's **feet** and keep swinging the rope underneath.

Step 1
Partner 1 sits on the ground face-to-face with partner 2, who is standing.

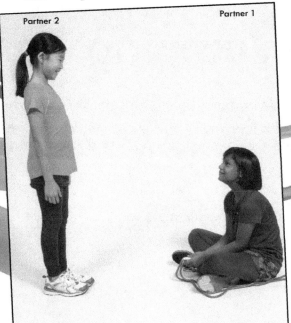

Partner 2   Partner 1

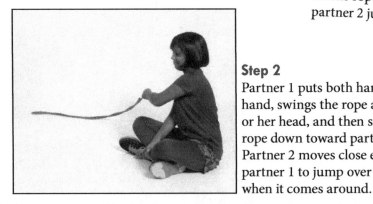

Step 3
As the rope comes down, partner 2 jumps over the rope.

Step 2
Partner 1 puts both handles in one hand, swings the rope around his or her head, and then swings the rope down toward partner 2's feet. Partner 2 moves close enough to partner 1 to jump over the rope when it comes around.

Verbal cues: partner 1 sits down   two handles in one hand   around your head and under

Jump and Slide
(Beginner)

This is the beginner's version of the Jump and Slide (page 148).

Helpful Hint:
Both partners will **always** be facing in the same direction, and the rope will **never** leave the ground.

Partner 2   Partner 1

Step 1
Each partner holds one handle in his or her right hand, and the partners stand side by side, facing in the same direction. Partner 1, who is on the right, jumps over the rope.

Step 2
Partner 1 slides left in front of partner 2 as partner 2 slides right. (They switch places.)

Step 3
Partner 2, who is now on the right, jumps over the rope. Repeat the Jump and Slide pattern.

Verbal cues: jump   and slide   jump

Jump Over, Jump Through
(Beginner)

This funtastic trick is our son Max's favorite trick!

Helpful Hint:
This trick is easier if the partner holding the rope is taller than the jumping partner.

As soon as partner 2 jumps over, partner 1 continues turning his or her body in a circle and begins to open his or her hands as wide as possible (one hand high, one hand low) to create a large loop. Partner 2 jumps through the loop when it comes around.

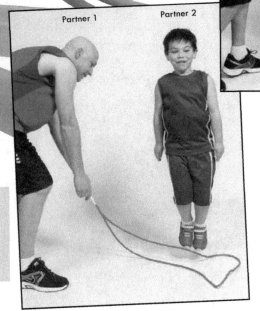

Partner 1   Partner 2

Step 1
Partner 1 holds one handle in each hand and faces partner 2. Partner 1 **slowly** begins to turn in a circle with both hands low so that the folded rope sweeps along the ground. When the rope comes near partner 2's feet, partner 2 jumps over the rope.

Step 3
Repeat the **jump over/jump through** pattern.

Verbal cues:	jump over	jump through	jump over

Cool Jump-Rope Tricks You Can Do

I Turn the Rope, You Turn in Circles
(Beginner)

This is one of the most popular partner jumping tricks. One partner turns the rope, and one partner just turns.

Helpful Hint:
The partner holding the rope needs to watch his or her partner's feet and get the rope underneath each jump.

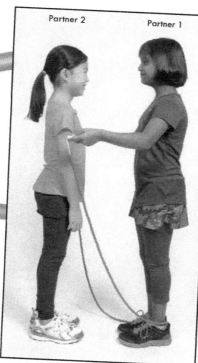

Step 1
Both partners stand face-to-face. Partner 1 holds one handle in each hand and the middle of the rope at his or her heels. Partner 1 tugs and taps.

Step 2
Partner 1 says, "Ready, set, go," and swings the rope over both partners' heads. Both partners begin jumping face-to-face.

Step 3
Once the partners have a rhythm down, partner 2 begins to turn around in a circle.

Verbal cues: jump together   turn in a circle

Side, Side, Open
(Intermediate)

This is a great trick to slowly speed up until you miss.

Helpful Hint:
The partner holding the rope should be able to do a 2-Hand Figure 8 (page 28) into an open jump (open side swing, crossed side swing, open jump) before adding partner 2.

Partner 1   Partner 2

Step 1
Partner 1 holds both handles of the rope. Partner 2 stands 10 feet behind partner 1. Partner 1 begins to do a 2-Hand Figure 8 (page 28) while partner 2 **carefully** moves forward to stand right behind partner 1.

Step 2
Partner 1 calls out (as the middle of the rope hits the ground each swing), "side" (on the open-side swing) "side" (on the crossed-side swing)…

Step 3
and then "open" (on the jump). Both partners jump over the rope on "jump." Repeat steps 2 and 3.

| Verbal cues: | side | side | open |

Side by Side
(Intermediate)

Here is the most popular partner jumping trick in which each partner holds one handle.

Helpful Hint:
Communicate and watch each other so that you start together and stay together.

Step 1
Both partners stand side by side, and each partner holds the rope in his or her outside hand.

Step 2
The partners both say, "Ready, set, go," and then both partners swing the rope over their head.

Step 3
Continue jumping.
Variation: What about side by side, facing in opposite directions?

Verbal cues: side by side   rope in outside hands   ready   set   go

The Mouse
(Intermediate)

This is another great partner trick to do with a big jumper (the turner) and a little jumper (the mouse).

Helpful Hint:

Partner 1 should slide both hands slightly to the right when partner 2 is on his or her right and both hands to the left when partner 2 is on his or her left.

Partner 2   Partner 1

Step 1
Partner 1 holds both handles and jumps face-to-face with partner 2.

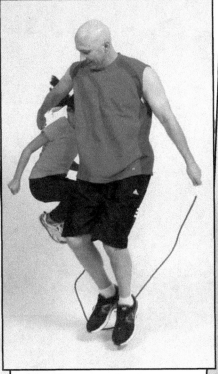

Step 2
Keeping the same rhythm, partner 2 begins to jump around partner 1.

Step 3
Partner 2 continues jumping all the way around partner 1.

Partner 2: Try to keep your shoulder close to partner 1 as you go around. You also may have to duck down a little when you go under partner 1's arms.

Verbal cues: jump together   go around

134   **Cool Jump-Rope Tricks You Can Do**

Jump to the Right, Turn to the Left
(Intermediate)

This is a new funtastic partner jumping trick that may leave you a little dizzy!

Helpful Hint:
Always turn left and keep the rope low!

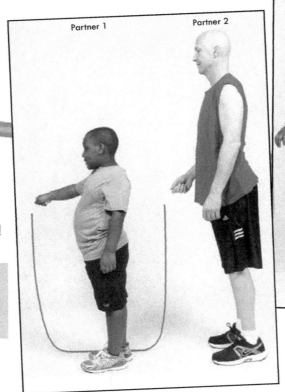

Partner 1   Partner 2

Step 1
Each partner holds one handle of the rope in his or her right hand. The two partners stand front to back, with the middle of the rope on the right side of partner 1.

Step 2
Partner 1 jumps over the rope to the right.

Step 3
Both partners begin to turn to the left.

Continued on next page.

Step 4
The partners keep turning left until the middle of the rope is on the right side of partner 2.

Step 5
Partner 2 jumps over the rope to the right.

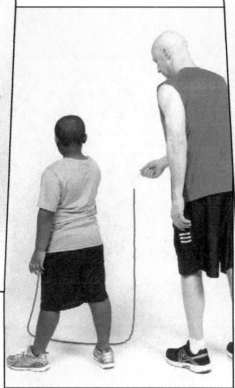

Step 6
Both partners begin to turn to the left.

Step 7
The partners keep turning left until the middle of the rope is on the right side of partner 1. Continue the "jump to the right, turn to the left" pattern.

jump to the right   turn to the left   jump to the right

Step 8
Start to swing the rope out to the side (keep the rope low) as both partners turn to the left.

Step 9
Partner 2 jumps over the rope.

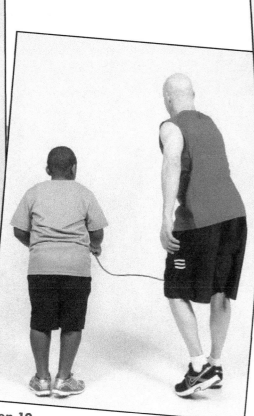

Step 10
Swing the rope out to the side (keep the rope low) as both partners turn to the left.

Step 11
Keep turning left. Partner 1 jumps over the rope. Repeat steps 8–11.

You Jump, I Jump
(Intermediate)

This is another one of my favorite partner jumping tricks to do. Even if one rope jumper is a beginner, this trick is still very doable.

Helpful Hint:
Let the less experienced jumper hold the rope in his or her strong hand.

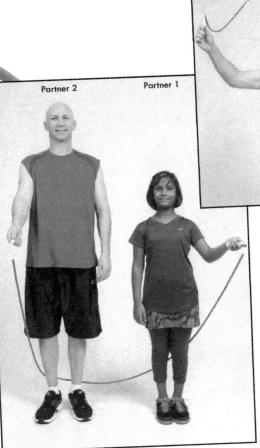

Partner 2   Partner 1

Step 2
Both partners say, "Ready, set, go," and then both partners swing the rope over their head.

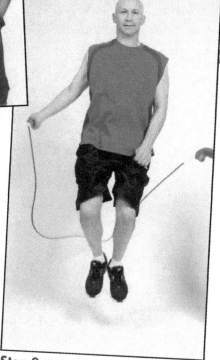

Step 1
Both partners stand side by side, facing the same direction. Each partner holds one handle of the rope and places the handle in his or her outside hand. The partners decide who will jump first.

Step 3
Partner 1 begins to cross his or her outside hand (the one that is holding the rope) toward partner 2, so that partner 2 can jump. Partner 2 jumps over the rope.

Verbal cues: side by side   pick who is jumping first   ready, set, go   you jump

Step 4
As the rope comes over partner 2's head, partner 1 begins to uncross as partner 2 begins to cross his or her outside hand over so that partner 1 can jump.

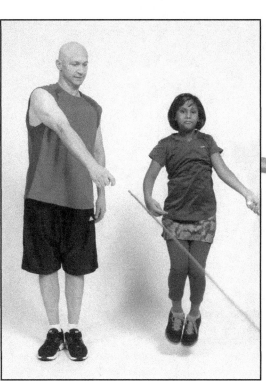

Step 5
Partner 2 continues to cross his or her arm in front while partner 1 prepares to jump.

Step 6
Partner 1 jumps over the rope.

Step 7
After partner 1 jumps and the rope comes over partner 1's head, partner 2 begins to uncross as partner 1 begins to cross his or her outside hand over so that partner 2 can jump. Repeat the You Jump/I Jump pattern.

You Jump/ I Jump, With a Crossed Jump

(Intermediate)

This is another variation on the You Jump/I Jump theme.

Helpful Hint:
Hold the end of the handle so that you can stick the handle out farther when you cross.

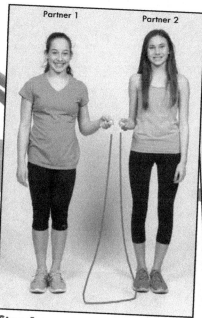

Step 1
Partner 1 and partner 2 stand side by side, and each one holds one handle of the rope in his or her inside hand.

Step 2
The partners say, "Ready, set, go," and swing the rope back and then forward over their heads. Partner 1 prepares to cross his or her arm and jump.

Step 3
Partner 1 crosses his or her hand to the outside and jumps.

Step 4
Partner 1 keeps turning with his or her arm crossed.

Step 5
As the rope comes down, partner 1 begins to uncross. Partner 2 begins to cross his or her arm.

Step 6
Partner 2 crosses his or her arm all the way to the outside and jumps.

Step 7
Partner 2 keeps turning with his or her arm crossed. Repeat the you jump/I jump pattern.

Back-to-Back
(Intermediate)

Here is a funtastic trick in which the rope goes **sideways** over your head.

Helpful Hint:
When you are turning the rope for this trick, pretend that you are drawing circles on a chalkboard out in front of you. **Steps 1–4 are preparation for the trick.**

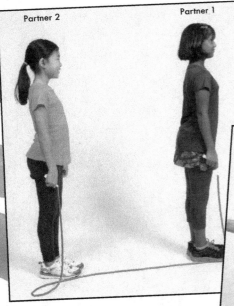

Partner 2   Partner 1

Step 1
Both partners face in the same direction, with each partner holding one handle of the rope in his or her right hand. Partner 1 stands a few feet in front of partner 2.

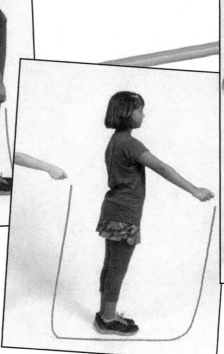

Step 2
Each partner extends his or her right arm forward so that the middle of the rope is on the ground just to the right of partner 1's right foot.

Step 3
The partners say, "Ready, set, go," and swing the rope sideways over partner 1's head.

Step 4
When the rope comes down, partner 1 jumps over it and continues jumping with the rope going sideways. Repeat steps 1–4 with partner 2 in front this time. Then both partners practice turning with either hand, in either direction.

Step 5
The partners stand back-to-back, with the rope on the side.

Stay back-to-back when you jump, but turn your head to the side where the rope is coming down.

Step 6
They extend their arms out. Then they say, "Ready, set, go." Then they swing the rope sideways over their head.

Step 7
The partners continue jumping (back-to-back, with the rope going sideways).

You Jump, I Jump 360 Inside Turn
(Intermediate)

First you turn when it's your turn to turn, then you jump. Got it?

Helpful Hint:
Make sure that you begin to turn inside, toward your partner, and continue to turn in that direction all the way around.

Step 1
Both partners stand side by side, facing the same direction. They both put the rope in their outside hand and tug.

Step 2
The partners say "Ready, set, go," and then they swing the rope over their heads.

Step 3
As the rope begins to come down, partner 1 turns toward partner 2. Partner 2 jumps.

Verbal cues: (given to the less experienced jumper)   turn all the way around

Step 4

As the rope comes over partner 2's head, partner 1 finishes the 360-degree turn. Partner 2 begins to turn toward Partner 1.

Step 5

As the rope begins to come down, partner 2 continues to turn (toward partner 1) and partner 1 (who has stopped turning for a moment) prepares to jump.

Step 6

Partner 2 continues turning in the same direction and sweeps the rope under partner 1's feet as he or she jumps.

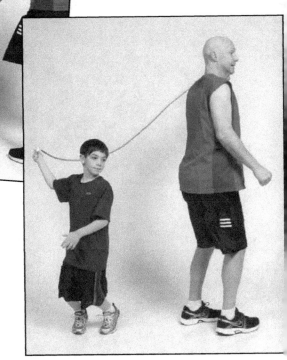

Step 7

As the rope comes over partner 1's head, partner 2 continues the 360-degree turn. Repeat steps 3–7.

and jump

Side by Slide
(Advanced)

Here is another partner jumping trick where one partner moves from his or her original position.

Helpful Hint:
It is usually easier for the taller partner to slide in back of the shorter partner.

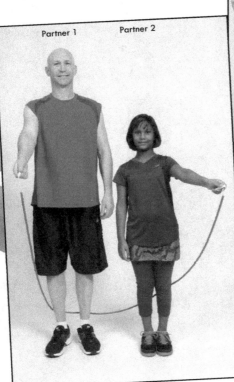

Partner 1   Partner 2

Step 1
Both partners stand side by side, facing in the same direction. Each partner holds one handle in his or her **outside** hand. The partners decide which of them will slide in back.

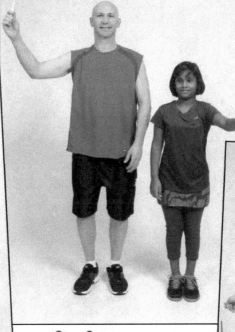

Step 2
Together, they say, "Ready, set, go," and swing the rope over their head.

Step 3
They jump together, side by side.

Verbal cues: side by side   rope in outside hands   ready, set, go   keep the rhythm

Partner 2 should hold the end of the handle. It will be easier for partner 1 to grab it and take it away.

Step 4
Keeping the same jumping rhythm, partner 1 begins to slide in back of partner 2.

Step 5
Partner 1 continues to slide in back of partner 2, until he or she is directly behind partner 2.

Step 6
Partner 1 **takes** the handle away from partner 2. Partner 2 should not try to hand the handle back to partner 1.

Step 7
Partner 1 now has both handles and continues turning. Both partners continue to jump together.

slide in back   take the handle

Partner Jumping Tricks

Jump and Slide
(Advanced)

Here is a partner jumping trick in which the rope basically stays in one place and the jumpers move around.

Helpful Hint:
TURN THE ROPE SLOWLY!

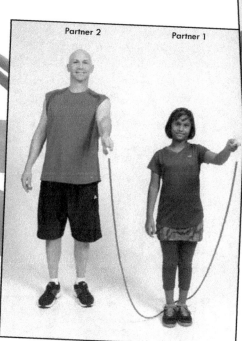

Partner 2   Partner 1

Step 1
Both partners stand side by side, and both face the same direction. Each partner puts one handle in his or her right hand. Place the rope behind partner 1. Partner 2 is to the left side of, and slightly behind, partner 1. Partner 2 will always be slightly behind partner 1.

Step 2
Both partners say, "Ready, set, go," and swing the rope over partner 1's head.

Step 3
As the rope comes down, partner 1 jumps as partner 2 gets ready to slide right.

Verbal cues: side by side   rope in right hands   ready, set, go   jump

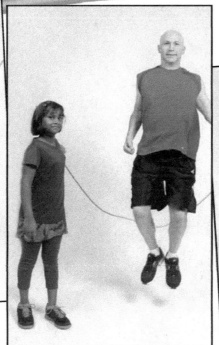

Step 4
As soon as partner 1 clears the rope, partner 2 slides right (in back of partner 1). As soon as partner 1 lands, partner 1 slides **left**. They change positions.

Both partners will always face the same direction.

Step 5
As the rope comes down, partner 2 jumps, and they prepare to slide and switch again.

Step 6
Partner 1 slides right as Partner 2 slides left. **TURN SLOWLY! MOVE QUICKLY!**

Step 7
Partner 1 jumps. Repeat steps 4–7.

and slide   jump   and slide   jump

The Scrambler
(Advanced)

This is my favorite funtastic partner jumping trick! The rope stays in one place and the jumpers scramble around!

Helpful Hint:
TURN THE ROPE SLOWLY!
Preparation: Partner 1 practices turning the rope **slowly**—counterclockwise, in his or her right hand—and jumping with the rope going sideways over his or her head. Then the partners switch positions so that partner 2 can practice the same thing.

Step 1
Each partner holds one handle of the rope in his or her right hand. They face in the same direction, and partner 1 stands a few feet in front and slightly to the left of partner 2 (just enough so that when partner 1 backs up and partner 2 moves forward, they won't run into each other). Each partner holds his or her right hand out in front. The middle of the rope should be touching the ground just to the right of partner 1's feet.

Step 2
Slowly swing the rope counterclockwise, sideways over partner 1's head. Partner 1 prepares to jump; partner 2 prepares to move forward.

Step 3
Partner 1 jumps over the rope.

Verbal cues: each hold one handle in your right hand   stand front to back   keep your hand in front   turn slowly

Both partners *always* face in the same direction and *always* keep their right hand out in front as they turn the rope.

Step 4
MOVE QUICKLY!
Partner 1 backs up and Partner 2 moves forward.

Step 5
When Partner 2 gets to the front position, partner 2 moves a little to the left and prepares to jump. As partner 1 gets to the back position, partner 1 moves a little to the right.

Step 6
Partner 2 jumps over the rope.

Step 7
As the rope passes in front of partner 1, partner 1 begins to move forward. After partner 2 lands, partner 2 moves straight back. As partner 1 gets to the front position, partner 1 moves a little to the left and partner 2 moves a little to the right. Repeat steps 3–7.

Also from Meadowbrook Press

✦ **Busy Books**

The Arts and Crafts Busy Book, *The Playdate Busy Book*, and *The Fitness Fun Busy Book* each contain hundreds of activities for your children, using items found around the home. The books offer parents and child-care providers fun reading, math, and science activities that will stimulate a child's natural curiosity. They also provide great activities for indoor play during even the longest stretches of bad weather! All four books show you how to save money by making your own paints, play dough, craft clays, glue, paste, and other arts-and-crafts supplies.

✦ **Giggle Poetry**

We know kids will love every one of our Giggle Poetry books, because kids picked every poem in them. Plus, we pack our anthologies with poems by the best poets around, like Kenn Nesbitt, Ted Scheu, Robert Pottle, Eric Ode, and Dave Crawley, as well as Bruce Lansky.

Kids Pick the Funniest Poems	*A Bad Case of the Giggles*
My Teacher's in Detention	*Miles of Smiles*
No More Homework! No More Tests!	*Rolling in the Aisles*
If Kids Ruled the School	*I Hope I Don't Strike Out!*
What I Did on My Summer Vacation	*I've Been Burping in the Classroom*

✦ *Giggle Poetry Reading Lessons*

Many struggling readers are embarrassed to read aloud. They are often intimidated or bored by texts that conventional programs require them to practice. So, instead of catching up, they fall further behind. "What is needed," Amy Buswell explains, "is a program that improves the motivation of struggling readers, because that accounts for 90% of the problem."

Four years ago, Buswell came up with a brainstorm. She knew her best readers enjoyed reading Bruce Lansky's poetry books for pleasure. The more poems they read, the better the reading got. Why not use Lansky's kid-tested poems as texts struggling readers could practice on to improve their reading.

This book is the result of that brainstorm and the resulting collaboration between Buswell and Lansky. It gives teachers and parents everything they need to help children improve their reading:

- 35 kid-tested poems by Bruce Lansky
- 35 customized reading lessons by Amy Buswell
- 35 off-the-wall illustrations by Stephen Carpenter
- 35 sets of zany performance tips by Bruce Lansky

…all of which is designed to make the process of reading improvement more like fun than work.

Also from The Rope Warrior

✦ **Ropenastics™ Workout DVD**

Burn Fat—Strengthen Muscles—Save Time

Learn the ropes as you hop, skip and jump your way to fitness! Join David, Lara, and Randi as they lead you through a fun, innovative, and challenging workout. Step-by-step, you'll learn basic skills that will enable you to do the Ropenastics™ workout and then be ready to create your own workout as you choose your intensity levels along the way.

Klutz to Professional Athlete: Ropenastics™ Is for Everyone!

Ropenastics™ is the ultimate total-body workout. You will amaze yourself as you improve your coordination, rhythm, cardiovascular endurance, foot speed, and leaping ability. It's also inexpensive, portable, and infinite in its creative possibilities.

✦ **Ropenastics™ Skills DVD**

An instructional jump-rope video for ages 5 and up

Learn over 50 jump-rope tricks to amaze your friends! It's like a private lesson from the world's greatest rope jumpers! Join David, Lori, and Sedric as they teach you "The Pretzel," "The Spinning Step-Through," "The Houdini," and lots of other cool tricks.

✦ **Jump Ropes**

All ropes are easy to turn, durable, and endorsed by the Rope Warrior.

Official Rope Warrior Speed Ropes: Make the air sing with your very own speed rope! Available in 7-foot length, 8-foot length, 9-foot length, 10-foot length, 14-foot length*, 16-foot length*.

Cloth Ropes: 14-foot length*, 16-foot length*.

Professional segmented jump rope: 9^1/$_2$-foot adjustable with padded handles.

*NOTE: Order 2 ropes for double Dutch.

✦ **Books**

Adventures of the Rope Warrior: A Legend is Launched

Charles "Skip" Roper is the sole survivor of a vicious alien attack on the Mars space station. Follow Skip as he leaps into the midst of interplanetary intrigue and searches the galaxy for the notorious leader of the Keebarian Space Chameleons.

Adventures of the Rope Warrior: Survival of the Fit

The Earth's entire existence hangs in the balance as Skip Roper returns in a mission against all odds in this second adventure-packed book.